THE REFERENCE SHELF   VOLUME 44 NUMBER 1

JUSTICE IN AMERICA

LAW, ORDER, AND THE COURTS

EDITED BY

WILLIAM P. LINEBERRY

Editor, The Council on Foreign Relations

THE H. W. WILSON COMPANY
NEW YORK   1972

THE REFERENCE SHELF

The books in this series contain reprints of articles, excerpts from books, and addresses on current issues and social trends in the United States and other countries. There are six separately bound numbers in each volume, all of which are generally published in the same calendar year. One number is a collection of recent speeches; each of the others is devoted to a single subject and gives background information and discussion from various points of view, concluding with a comprehensive bibliography. Books in the series may be purchased individually or on subscription.

Library of Congress Cataloging in Publication Data

Lineberry, William P   comp.
    Justice in America.

    (The Reference shelf, v. 44, no. 1)
    Bibliography: p.
    1. Criminal justice, Administration of—U. S.
—Addresses, essays, lectures. I. Title. II. Series.
KF9223.A75L5   345'.73'05   75-39399
ISBN 0-8242-0464-6

PREFACE

For many Americans, and especially for those of us living in the nation's larger cities, the breakdown of the American system of justice now seems complete. With the streets unsafe for law-abiding citizens, with policemen being gunned down by criminal elements (fifty-one killed in the first five months of 1971 alone), with one out of five crimes going unsolved, and with trials of the accused lagging anywhere from six months to a year behind schedule—until memories fade, witnesses move or die, and victims lose interest in the redress of their own grievances—with, in short, justice delayed, denied, and derided to an extent unprecedented in our history, there are few of us, indeed, who any longer place faith in that credo carved above the entrance to the highest court in the land: "Equal Justice Under Law." As Deputy Attorney General Richard G. Kleindienst sums the problem up, the American system of criminal justice is in a state of collapse: "It is failing to deter criminals. It is failing to restrain criminals. It is failing to rehabilitate criminals."

Not surprisingly, in such circumstances, crime rates go right on climbing, as the annual reports of the Federal Bureau of Investigation remind us year after year, placing an ever greater strain on an already overburdened system. The cycle seems vicious and unending. Rising crime in the streets adds to the crisis already underway in the courts. Overworked judges turn those accused of crime back out upon the streets (nine out of ten never go to trial), where many of them renew the unequal contest with overworked police; or the judges pack the guilty off to overcrowded and understaffed prisons, where unrehabilitated convicts are prematurely released to make way for the ever-rising tide of newcomers. As it stands, the system seems almost ironically designed to entrap the innocent, encourage the guilty, and

3

leave the public at large without adequate recourse or protection.

Is there a way out of this cycle? What can be done to improve our system of justice, to protect the innocent, rehabilitate the guilty, and restore a sense of safety to the streets of our cities? With the "law-and-order" issue a chief element in almost every politician's campaign for office, the time for complacency about such problems seems well past. In its outrage over the issue, the public itself has been lashing out—now at the Supreme Court for its alleged "permissiveness," now at the police for their alleged brutality and corruption, now at the prisons for their failure to reform (or repress) those in their charge, and now at society itself for providing the breeding grounds in which poverty, crime, and injustice can thrive.

Rarely are such monumental problems subject to easy solution, and more rarely still is there general agreement about what precisely needs to be done. There are those who believe that more money spent on courts, police, and prisons would go a long way toward resolving the crisis, but there are also those who think such money might be better spent in rooting out the poverty, prejudice, and injustice upon which crime feeds. There are those who believe quite literally that too many criminals are getting away with murder, that leniency in the application of the law has encouraged disrespect for the law, and that what is needed is a tougher measure of law and order, generally. And there are those who see the failure to protect the innocent and administer truly equal justice to rich and poor alike as the greatest injustice of all, undermining the foundations not only of respect for the law but of individual rights and liberties as well.

The purpose of this volume is to examine the highly besieged state of justice in America today, to set forth the main controversies surrounding it, and to explore the key proposals being made as means of reform. The first section sets the framework for the discussion—tracing the origins and development of criminal law at the state and local level;

reflecting on the causes of lawlessness in America, and de-
lineating two general, if opposing, approaches to the cure;
defining the scope and dimensions of the current problems
in need of solution; and marking out in broad strokes the
reasons a crisis is at hand. Section II focuses on the special
troubles besetting the courts. If in theory the judiciary should
be the proud centerpiece in the American system of justice,
in practice it is in distress, unable to cope with its traditional
task of administering the law swiftly and equitably and prevented, largely by lack of funds, from doing anything to
relieve its plight. As though overcrowded calendars, delayed
trials, and insufficient personnel were not enough to contend
with, the courts have also become a prime target of ideological attack by those in revolt not only against the American system of justice but against the American system in
general. Today's judges must be prepared to confront unruly defendants whose contempt for the system verges on
contempt for the judges themselves.

The third section sets forth the views of those who believe
that the American system of justice is threatened most by
its failure to protect the rights and liberties of individuals
and to accord equal treatment to minorities automatically
suspect because of skin color or foreign origin, and by its
often rough and sometimes callous disregard of the poor.
As former Attorney General Ramsey Clark describes one
key problem: "The bail system is worse than senseless—it
discriminates for no reason against the poor. Bail diverts
the criminal justice system from what matters—the individual
—to what doesn't—his money."

The fourth section takes up the viewpoint of those who
have come to be called the law-and-order advocates. Aware
as they are of the many constitutional and legal safeguards
for individual rights, they want to know who will protect
a society besieged by crime. Perhaps nothing reveals so keen-
ly the general state of disarray into which our system of
justice has fallen as James Mills' scathing description in
this section of a few days in the life of a Legal Aid Society

defense attorney and of the cynicism that alone, perhaps, keeps the wheels of justice spinning.

The last section looks to the future and examines in some detail the kinds of reforms currently proposed or going into effect. The success or failure of these proposals will determine the fate of American justice.

The compiler wishes to thank the authors and publishers who have courteously granted permission for the reprinting of their materials in this book. He is especially indebted to Stephanie Lineberry for her generous and able assistance in the preparation of the manuscript.

WILLIAM P. LINEBERRY

January 1972

CONTENTS

I. AMERICAN JUSTICE IN PERSPECTIVE

EDITOR'S INTRODUCTION

The American system of justice is a sprawling, complex entity embracing some 40,000 Federal, state, and local law enforcement agencies, of which 39,750 are local. Such complexity can be a source of trouble in itself, although the many levels and varieties of courts were designed originally to protect the innocent as well as to serve the needs of an increasingly expanding and varied society. Almost everyone agrees that this massive system is now in need of massive repairs. Whether the watchwords be "equal justice impartially administered" or "law and order," few seem to believe that the present system is performing its task truly and well.

The evidence abounds. Mountainous backlogs of both criminal and civil cases demonstrate the old maxim "justice delayed is justice denied." Some courts are so jammed that proceedings must take place in the judges' robing rooms. The system has been under severe strain for many years, as America's population has grown and concentrated itself in high-crime urban areas. As crime rates rose, so did the number of laws on the books and so did the number of Supreme Court decisions granting more protection to persons accused of crime. Judges already swamped with divorce cases, damage suits arising from automobile accidents, and medical malpractice suits were to be overwhelmed with civil-rights and consumer-protection actions and more cases arising out of environmental issues and the growing use of narcotics. The backlogs increased and a crisis arose. A system designed for another, simpler, era was collapsing in the face of the new.

This section is designed to familiarize the reader with the background of our system of justice and to outline current problems. The first article traces the somewhat haphazard origins and development of law enforcement in the United States, from the days of the night watchmen who served Colonial society to the present technologically sophisticated and highly integrated complex of Federal, state, and local agencies. Next, the noted historian Henry Steele Commager examines the roots of lawlessness in America, concluding somewhat reassuringly that we have always been a violent people but warning nonetheless that the values which have kept violence at bay in the past are now in danger of being eroded.

In the third article, Richard L. Strout of the *Christian Science Monitor* surveys the approach of the Nixon Administration to law-and-order issues and contrasts it to the recommendations of four recent presidential commissions looking into the best means of fighting crime. The fourth article reports some of the provocative views set forth by experts during the Congressional Conference on Justice in America in 1970. The concluding article of the section, from *Senior Scholastic,* explains graphically why our system of justice is under heavy fire today.

ORIGINS AND DEVELOPMENT OF AMERICAN LAW ENFORCEMENT [1]

The development of local and state law enforcement in this country has followed a long, slow and tortuous path —a path that leads back to early English history.

The Saxons brought to England a tribal system of justice which relied heavily on community organization. People were divided into groups of families in tens, called "tythings," headed by a "tything man," and into larger groups, each of ten tythings, under a "hundred-man" who was responsible to the "shire-reeve" (sheriff) of the county. Thus

[1] "Development of Local and State Law Enforcement," by Virgil W. Peterson, visiting lecturer, University of Illinois, Chicago Circle Campus; formerly executive director, Chicago Crime Commission. *Current History.* 60:327-34. Je. '71. Reprinted by permission of Current History, Inc.

each person was accountable to his group for observing the laws, and the group, in turn, was responsible for the individual's law-abiding behavior.

Following the Norman conquest in 1066, the Anglo-Saxon shires and hundreds were continued for the purpose of local administration and for local justice under the sheriffs, who were subject to removal by the king. The communities were held responsible for maintaining order, and the sheriff was an essential link between them and the central government. Eventually, the tithing man became the parish constable and gradually many of the functions of the sheriff were transferred to the Knights of the Shire who, in time, became justices of the peace. The constable, as representative of the people of the parish, was responsible to the justice of the peace.

In each parish, an unarmed, able-bodied citizen was appointed or elected to serve as constable without pay for one year. In the towns, the responsibility for law and order was vested not only in the constable and the citizens generally, but in the guilds and other groups who supplied bodies of men known as "The Watch" to guard the gates and patrol the streets at night.

Citizens increasingly objected to performing the somewhat onerous and dangerous duties required of a constable. Eventually, the right to appoint paid deputies to serve in their stead was granted. The deputy constables developed into a professional class who sold their services to one citizen after another. Often they worked in league with the lawless elements. Corruption was prevalent. And the night watchmen appointed to patrol the streets were frequently feeble elderly men unfit for other work.

The American Colonies

It was the sheriff-constable-watchman system that the colonists transplanted to American shores following their settlement early in the seventeenth century. From this base there evolved the forty-thousand separate and independent police forces in the United States today.

Forerunners of present-day police forces in this country were parish constables and night watchmen appointed by the colonists to patrol the streets of towns at night and to cry out the time and give the state of the weather.

In 1636, a night watch was established in Boston and before long almost every settlement in New England had at least a few watchmen. Even in the Dutch town of New Amsterdam, later New York City, an ordinance was passed on April 29, 1654, providing for the establishment of a "rattle-watch" of from four to six men to guard the city at night. Because of a lack of response on the part of the residents, the watch was not placed into actual operation until October 1658. After English rule was established, the Dongan charter of 1686 provided for a high constable, subconstables and watchmen. Exercising supervision over the watchmen were the constables elected from the various wards. In Philadelphia, a night watchman was appointed by the provincial council in 1700 and a system was initiated which required all citizens to take turns in performing watch duties. In Boston, following a petition to the general court in 1762, an act was passed which gave the selectmen the right to choose a number of inhabitants, not to exceed thirty, to serve as watchmen. This provision, later reenacted, remained in force until Boston became a city in 1822.

In the early 1800s, it became increasingly apparent that the night watch was inadequate to meet the needs of the time. The ranks of the professional watchmen were comprised largely of men who were employed at other jobs during the day time. Their selection was based on political considerations. The watch was organized by wards and districts, each operating independently of the other. In New York City, the watch service extended from 9 P.M. to sunrise and some watch captains interpreted sunrise at 3 A.M. while others insisted it was 5 A.M.

In Philadelphia, the will of Stephen Girard bequeathed a large sum of money to finance a competent police force for the city. As a result, an ordinance, passed in 1833, provided for a force of 24 policemen to serve in the day as well as 120 watchmen to serve at night. The control of the force was centralized in one officer, a captain, and eliminated the chaos which had stemmed from the district autonomy prevailing up to that time. However, only two years later, this ordinance was repealed and the city returned to the old system of district independence.

In 1838, Boston adopted a plan of forming a day force of six watchmen. Within eight years this force had grown to thirty. There was no connection, however, between the day force and the night watch of 150 men. In 1842, Cincinnati created a day watch of two men selected by the council. Eight years later the council provided for the election by popular vote of six day watchmen for each of the city's wards. In 1844, the day watch in New York City was comprised of 16 officers appointed by the mayor in addition to 108 for Sunday duty. The night watch, consisting of 1,100 watchmen, was completely separate from the day force. A third force in New York City was made up of 100 "mayor's marshals" who, with 34 constables of whom two were elected from each ward, served as general peace officers.

In city after city, friction existed between two independent police forces—one for day and the other for night. It was an impossible arrangement, totally incapable of coping with increasing lawlessness in the cities. In 1844, the New York legislature passed an act which created a unified "day and night" force of eight hundred men for New York City and abolished the watch system altogether. Supervision of the force was vested in a chief of police, to be appointed by the mayor with the consent of the council. Opposition to the act by local officials resulted in much bickering and confusion for five months but on May 23, 1845, an ordinance was passed by the city fathers making the act effective. This action in New York formed the basis for modern police organization in the United States. Police forces under a single head were created in Chicago in 1851, in New Orleans and Cincinnati in 1852, in Baltimore and Newark in 1857 and in Providence in 1864. In Boston, the night watch which had been in existence over two hundred years was consolidated with the day force in 1854 and a department of 250 men was created under the control of a chief of police to be appointed by the mayor.

Partisan Politics

The movement to consolidate day and night police forces under a single head, known as a chief or marshal, was a highly significant step in the development of police organization in American cities. But the road ahead to create efficient municipal police departments was long and rocky. And a principal stumbling block was partisan politics.

Under the New York law of 1844, policemen as well as their superior officers were appointed for one year only following nomination to their posts by aldermen and assistant aldermen of the wards to which they belonged. The chief of police was largely a figurehead with little, if any, authority over his force, a situation that has prevailed in many cities until modern times. It was a common practice for political parties in power to use their police forces to control elections.

During the 1850s it was not uncommon for cities to provide for the popular election of the police department chief or marshal. This was true in Philadelphia, San Francisco, Chicago and Cleveland. In Brooklyn, the people not only elected the chief of police but the captains as well.

It is not surprising that the heads of police departments were unable to maintain necessary discipline. Officers commonly defied departmental regulations and occasionally assaulted their superiors. For a long time there was great resistance to wearing uniforms. By 1855, a few communities required regulation hats and caps but no city at that time had a completely uniformed force. And when the New York City police required uniforms in 1856, each ward decided on its own style.

Following the movement to consolidate day and night police forces, the departments of most cities were controlled by city councils for the greater part of a decade. In 1850, the administrative control of the Philadelphia department was vested in a police board consisting of the marshal and the presidents of town boards of communities within the police district. In 1853, New York City created an administrative body called the Board of Police Commissioners, comprised of the mayor, recorder and city judge. For the next forty-eight years, the New York City department was in the hands of some form of police board.

Following the example of Philadelphia and New York City, other municipalities that created administrative boards with control over their police departments were New Orleans, in 1853, Cincinnati and San Francisco, in 1859, Detroit, St. Louis and Kansas City, in 1861, Buffalo and Cleveland, in 1866. In the decade beginning in 1870, almost all important cities experimented with some kind of police board.

Police departments were generally inefficient; often corrupt. Frequently action by state legislatures to create boards to administer police departments was based on political considerations—struggles for power between state administrations controlled by one party and city administrations dominated by the other party.

By an act of the New York legislature on April 15, 1857, New York, Kings, Westchester and Richmond counties were combined into a Metropolitan Police District under the administration of a board of five commissioners appointed by the governor. The mayors of New York City and Brooklyn were ex-officio members of the board but they were subject to removal by the governor. Fernando Wood, mayor of New York City, refused to recognize the authority of the state-appointed police commissioners and on June 16, 1857, there was an open clash at city hall between members of the new

Metropolitan force and the existing municipal department. Military forces were called in to quell the battle. Within a short time, the courts upheld the legality of the new Metropolitan Police District and Mayor Wood capitulated. In the interim, however, whenever a member of the Metropolitan force arrested a criminal, an officer of the municipal department would release him. And members of the two rival forces would battle each other with their clubs while the offender proceeded on his way unmolested.

The Illinois state legislature, in February 1861, enacted a law which established state control over the Chicago Police Department through the creation of a Board of three police commissioners. The board held its first meeting on the night of March 21, 1861. Chicago's mayor, Long John Wentworth, in defiance of the new law, summoned all men on the city force to his office at 2 A.M. and discharged them. Chicago, then overrun with criminals, was left with no police protection at all for a short time.

Ostensibly, the purpose of placing the management of local police departments in state-controlled boards was to eliminate the influence of politics. In general, this goal was not achieved and there was much objection to state control because it violated the principle of local autonomy—home rule. By 1915, 12 of 23 cities having a population in excess of 250,000 had experimented with state-controlled police systems. By 1920, such systems had survived in only four—Baltimore, Boston, Kansas City and St. Louis.

In 1931, the Wickersham Commission concluded that the underlying causes for general police ineffectiveness were the politicians' control of the chief which resulted in his insecurity and short term in office and the political favoritism which prevailed in the selection of patrolmen and other personnel. The commission related instances where underworld elements such as gamblers, through their political alliances, had named the chiefs of police of several large cities. In others, competent chiefs of police had been removed by the same influences. In the city of Detroit there had been four police heads in the preceding year. In Chicago, there were fourteen chiefs of police in thirty years and the average tenure of office for police heads in cities of 500,000 population was only a fraction over two years. Under such conditions, the development of outstanding leadership from within the ranks and the building of sound police organizations based on careful planning were virtually impossible.

An effective police operation includes not only competent personnel working under sound management policies but an efficient communications system and the equipment necessary to patrol the streets and pursue offenders. The Wickersham Commission reported in 1931 that based on its study, with perhaps two exceptions, not a single police force in cities above 300,000 population had "an adequate communication system and equipment essential . . . to meet the criminal on even equal terms."

During the first two decades of the present century, the central siren, the telephone and call box constituted the sole means of communication between patrolmen on the street and headquarters. Some departments had a bell, a light or a horn installed on top of the call box to summon officers. A further advance in communications was the development of the teletype system. But the most important police communication system involved the radio. With the advent of the radio-equipped police car late in the 1920s there arrived a new era in police communication.

The first practical police radio installation was inaugurated in Detroit in 1928. A national study in 1931 disclosed that of cities in excess of 500,000 population, only one, Detroit, had police radio equipment and of all other cities of over 10,000 people, there were only three with such police installations. Of 390 cities studied, only 34 were equipped with teletype reception instruments.

Today, there are few departments in cities of any size, as well as county and rural departments, that do not have police radio equipment. The development of efficient communication systems since 1930 has been phenomenal. For

the year 1929, it was considered a remarkable feat that the
Detroit department made 22,598 broadcasts which resulted
in 1,325 arrests. In 1967, the Federal Bureau of Investigation
established a National Crime Information Center in Washington, D.C., which maintains a computerized index of
documented police information that is made available to
all law-enforcement agencies. At the end of the fiscal year
1970, the entries in the master computer totaled 2,032,150.
On a single day, 63,246 transactions were handled and, at
times, the hourly rate of messages from police departments
located in all sections of the country exceeded 3,000.

The development of a systematic plan to transmit criminal information throughout the United States had been a
principal subject of discussion when the administrators of
police departments held their first general conference in
St. Louis in 1871. Other matters of primary concern were
identification systems, criminal statistics and the formation
of a permanent National Police Association which was re-
organized in 1893 as the International Association of Chiefs
of Police (IACP).

A National Clearinghouse

A national clearinghouse for criminal identification records was established by IACP in 1896. The records consisted
of photographs of known criminals and a system of anthropo-
metric measurements devised by the French criminologist,
Alphonse Bertillon, in 1882. Originally, the clearinghouse
records were maintained in Chicago. After 1904, the Bertillon
system was gradually replaced by fingerprints.

During the early years of the national bureau of criminal
identification, it was supported by fees from less than 150
police forces and an occasional congressional appropriation
of $500. This represented the first systematic attempt at
cooperative activity in United States police work.

The IACP entered into negotiations to have the Federal
Government maintain the national identification bureau

which was set up in 1924. The records of the national bureau were consolidated with those of Federal prisoners maintained at Leavenworth, Kansas, and were transferred to Washington, D.C., under the jurisdiction of the FBI, where the fingerprint collection grew into the largest in the world.

Although the compilation of crime statistics was of concern to the National Police Association at its first meeting in 1871, over a half century passed before a successful project was launched. In 1927, the IACP organized a Committee on Uniform Crime Records, and a system of uniform crime statistics was developed. The first returns in January 1930, included four hundred police jurisdictions located in forty-three states. On July 31, 1930, the entire system of uniform crime reports was transferred by the IACP to the FBI, which assumed the role as the national clearinghouse and has published regular reports since that time.

Scientific crime detection laboratories were virtually unknown when police administrators first gave attention to the need for adequate crime statistics, communication and identification systems. Crime laboratories had their origin in Europe and the first well-equipped police science laboratory was established on this continent in 1929 by private interests in Chicago working through Northwestern University. After a few years, the Northwestern University laboratory was acquired by the Chicago Police Department and major police departments throughout the country began establishing laboratories with technical staffs. Since 1933, the extensive facilities of the FBI laboratory in Washington, D.C., have been made available to police agencies throughout the nation.

The American police were also slow to recognize the need for training programs. It was not until 1920 that training programs became common. In 1931, the Wickersham Commission reported that the establishment of the police school was perhaps the most important change that had taken place in the police world during the preceding thirty-five years. Yet, at that time in cities with a population under ten thousand, nothing was being done which "by any stretch of the imagination could be considered police training." In 1935, the FBI established the National Police Academy. Its extensive courses are attended by officers from all parts of the nation. One of its primary goals is to train instructors attached to local and state police schools. In recent years, police training has made rapid progress. Outstanding police academies have been established in some of the major cities. Inadequate training programs are still problems in many of the smaller municipalities.

The major burden for maintaining law and order in American cities and urban centers rests with our police departments. They have developed their present status largely without plan. Their structures represent a patchwork—the addition of a division here and a service there to meet some pressing need of the time.

In consequence, the quality of police service varies from city to city—some are inept and inefficient; others will compare favorably with the finest in the world. All had their origin in the English sheriff-constable system of Colonial days. And as the United States became more and more urbanized, the sheriff as well as the constable deteriorated in significance as a factor in the overall law enforcement picture in this country.

About 40 percent of the constitutions of our fifty states give recognition to the office of constable. Legally, there are more separate and distinct police units constructed around the office of constable than any other type. Yet the law enforcement activities of the constable have largely lapsed. In some places the citizens do not bother to elect constables because no one will accept the offices. Even in rural counties in some states, such as Illinois and New York, most constables perform no police duties of any kind. In smaller villages, the fee-compensated constable has been displaced by the full-time village policeman. At the present time, the office of constable has virtually no impact insofar as law enforcement is concerned.

Office of Sheriff

In county government, the sheriff is the principal law-enforcement officer. Once the Anglo-Saxon king's steward, he was deprived of many of his judicial powers by the Magna Carta in 1215. By the beginning of the sixteenth century, the justices of the peace had secured control of local police systems in England and thereafter the law-enforcement powers of the sheriff were progressively trimmed until they virtually disappeared.

The early American sheriff was a landed proprietor and his office was one of honor as well as profit. Since the United States was founded, the sheriff's office has been elective. Thus, the principal law-enforcement officer of the county is directly involved in partisan politics.

The golden days of the sheriff occurred as the frontiers of America swept westward. His exploits in engaging in gunplay with outlaws and leading a posse to capture desperadoes were widely heralded and became embedded in the traditions of the Wild West.

Today, in many places the sheriff performs few, if any, law-enforcement duties but confines himself to caring for the county jail and serving civil processes. In counties in which cities are located, the sheriff usually engages in law-enforcement work only beyond the municipal boundaries or on rare occasions when the city police specifically request his aid.

In 1931, the Wickersham Commission noted that partisan politics dictate the appointment of personnel to the sheriff's office. And with the handful of deputies to aid him, it was impossible for the sheriff to maintain any kind of adequate patrol. The commission concluded that "while there may be isolated examples of competent forces under this plan they are, at present, rare, and can hardly be expected to become the model for an extensive system." (United States. National Commission on Law Observance & Enforcement.

Report on Police, No. 14. Supt. of Docs., Washington, D.C.
20025. '31. p 128.)

At the present time in the United States, there are 3,050
counties, each with a sheriff's office. These range in size from
a one-man force in Putnam County, Georgia, to a 5,515-man
force in Los Angeles. Of the 3,050 sheriff's offices, only 200
have a staff of more than fifty officers.

A number of sheriff's offices have developed competent
highway patrols with full law-enforcement powers. And in
some places there have been created county police forces
that operate independently of the sheriff's office. This is true
of the Nassau County Police Department in New York,
which was established in 1925 and is the second largest police
force in the state.

At the state level of government, the dominant law-enforcement agencies are state police or highway patrols. Such
organizations exist in all states except Hawaii.

Statewide police agencies were slow to develop in the
United States. In some respects, the forerunner of present-
day state police forces were the Texas Rangers, organized in
1835 by the provisional government of Texas. Originally,
three Ranger companies were formed under the direction
of the military service to guard the borders, a function that
was performed for many years. Eventually, criminal investigation became a principal activity of the Rangers, and in
1935 the Texas Department of Safety took over control of
this highly publicized force.

In 1865, Massachusetts appointed a few constables with
statewide powers to suppress vice. Since they were granted
general police powers throughout the state, Massachusetts
may be credited with having established the first state police
force. Following recurrent legislation, the Massachusetts
District of Police, a state detective unit, was formed in 1879.
In 1903, Connecticut formed a small state force to suppress
commercialized vice. Gradually it acquired the characteristics
of a state detective force.

The Origins of the Modern State Police

The establishment of the Pennsylvania State Police in 1905 marked the beginning of modern state police organization in this country. Governor Pennypacker, who became the chief executive in 1903, learned that while he had the duty to enforce the state laws, he was without any instrument to carry out his responsibilities. He therefore created the state police to serve as a general executive arm for the state, to cope with disturbed conditions in the coal and iron regions which local law enforcement officers had demonstrated an incapacity to handle, and to provide police protection in the rural districts where the sheriff-constable system had broken down.

The new superintendent of the state police was responsible only to the governor. His force, a mounted and uniformed body, operated out of troop headquarters and substations and adopted a policy of providing continuous patrol throughout the rural areas. It also pioneered in the field of police training. It was the first force in the country to provide a systematic police training program for its recruits.

The Pennsylvania State Police served as a pattern for the creation of state police organizations in several states. This was true of the New York State Police which was formed in 1917. The same year the Michigan State Police was hastily organized as a war measure and it acquired permanent status in 1919. Also formed in 1919 was a state police force in West Virginia.

In 1920, Massachusetts took steps to consolidate into the Department of Public Safety all state agencies, including its detective units, that had any relationship to public safety. At the same time it established a statewide, uniformed patrol force patterned after the Pennsylvania State Police. State police forces were also formed in New Jersey in 1921 and in Rhode Island in 1925.

In 1927, Connecticut completed a series of changes which brought its state force more nearly into line with Pennsylvania. In 1929, a state force in Maine which had been created specifically to enforce the motor vehicle laws had its powers extended to include the maintenance of general police patrols and to conduct criminal investigations throughout the state.

The creation of state forces with general law-enforcement powers met with substantial opposition in many places, particularly from labor unions. Today, there are state police forces in twenty-five states and state highway patrols in twenty-four. The highway patrols are largely restricted to traffic law enforcement and conducting accident prevention programs. At the beginning of 1970, the forty-nine state police and highway patrols had a total personnel of 52,812.

At every level of government, there are special-purpose law-enforcement agencies that are independent of the traditional local and state police forces. They add to the problems of fragmentation, frequent duplicating and overlapping agencies which characterize the law-enforcement structure all over the United States.

Of 40,000 Federal, state and local law-enforcement agencies in the United States, 39,750 are local. And the full-time personnel of local law enforcement comprises 83 percent of the total. Obviously, throughout its history, the United States has continued to adhere to the old Anglo-Saxon tradition which relied heavily on local, community organization in law-enforcement matters.

THE ROOTS OF LAWLESSNESS [2]

It was in 1838 that the young Abraham Lincoln—he was not yet twenty-nine—delivered an address at Springfield, Illinois, on "The Perpetuation of Our Political Institutions." What he had to say is curiously relevant today. Like many of us, Lincoln was by no means sure that our institutions

[2] From article by Henry Steele Commager, professor of history at Amherst College, author of many books and articles on American history and social questions. Saturday Review. 54:17-19+. F. 13, '71. Copyright 1971 Saturday Review, Inc. Reprinted by permission of the author and Saturday Review.

could be perpetuated; unlike some of us, he was convinced that they should be.

What, after all, threatened American political institutions? There was no threat from outside, for "all the armies of Europe, Asia, and Africa combined could not by force take a drink from the Ohio or make a track on the Blue Ridge in a thousand years." No, the danger was from within. "If destruction be our lot, we must ourselves be its author and finisher. As a nation of freemen, we must live through all time or die by suicide."

This, Lincoln asserted, was not outside the realm of possibility; as he looked about him, he saw everywhere a lawlessness that, if persisted in, would surely destroy both law and Constitution and eventually the nation itself. In the end, lawlessness *did* do that—lawlessness in official guise that refused to abide by the constitutional processes of election or by the will of the constitutional majority. It was to be Lincoln's fate to be called upon to frustrate that lawless attack on the nation, and to be remembered as the savior of the Union. And it has been our fate to be so bemused by that particular threat to unity—the threat of sectional fragmentation—that we have failed to appreciate the danger that so deeply disturbed Lincoln at the threshold of his political career. . . .

We are tempted to say of Lincoln's Springfield address that it was short-sighted of him not to have seen that the threats to union were slavery and sectionalism—something he learned, in time. We should say rather that he was far-sighted in imagining the possibility of a very different threat to union: an internal dissension and lawlessness that bespoke a breakdown in cultural and moral unity. This is what confronts us today: blacks against whites, old against young, skinheads against eggheads, militarists against doves, the cities against the suburbs and the countryside—hostilities that more and more frequently erupt into open violence.

Two considerations warrent attention. First, that what Lincoln described was in fact normal—we have always been a lawless and a violent people. Thus, our almost unbroken record of violence against the Indians and all others who got in our way—the Spaniards in the Floridas, the Mexicans in Texas; the violence of the vigilantes on a hundred frontiers; the pervasive violence of slavery (a "perpetual exercise," Jefferson called it, "of the most boisterous passions"); the lawlessness of the Ku Klux Klan during Reconstruction and after; and of scores of race riots from those of New Orleans in the 1860s to those of Chicago in 1919. Yet, all this violence, shocking as it doubtless was, no more threatened the fabric of our society or the integrity of the Union than did the lawlessness of Prohibition back in the twenties. The explanation for this is to be found in the embarrassing fact that most of it was official, quasi-official, or countenanced by public opinion: exterminating the Indian: flogging the slave; lynching the outlaw; exploiting women and children in textile mills and sweatshops; hiring Pinkertons to shoot down strikers; condemning immigrants to fetid ghettos; punishing Negroes who tried to exercise their civil or political rights. Most of this was socially acceptable—or at least not wholly unacceptable—just as so much of our current violence is socially acceptable: the 50,000 automobile deaths every year; the mortality rate for Negro babies twice that for white; the deaths from cancer induced by cigarettes or by air pollution; the sadism of our penal system and the horrors of our prisons; the violence of the police against what Theodore Parker called the "perishing and dangerous classes of society."

The New Polarization

What we have now is the emergence of violence that is not acceptable either to the Establishment, which is frightened and alarmed, or to the victims of the Establishment, who are no longer submissive and who are numerous and powerful. This is the now familar "crime in the streets," or it is the revolt of the young against the economy, the politics, and the wars of the established order, or it is the

convulsive reaction of the blacks to a century of injustice.
But now, too, official violence is no longer acceptable to its
victims—or to their ever more numerous sympathizers: the
violence of great corporations and of government itself
against the natural resources of the nation; the long-drawn-
out violence of the white majority against Negroes and other
minorities; the violence of the police and the National Guard
against the young; the massive and never-ending violence
of the military against the peoples of Vietnam and Cambodia. These acts can no longer be absorbed by large segments of our society. It is this new polarization that threatens
the body politic and the social fabric much as religious dissent threatened them in the Europe of the sixteenth and
seventeenth centuries.

A second consideration is this: The center of gravity has
shifted from "obedience" to "enforcement." This shift in
vocabulary is doubtless unconscious but nonetheless revealing. Obedience is the vocabulary of democracy, for it rec-
ognizes that the responsibility for the commonwealth is in
the people and appeals to the people to recognize and fulfill
their responsibility. Enforcement is the language of authority prepared to impose its will on the people. Lincoln knew
instinctively that a democracy flourishes when men obey
and revere the law; he did not invoke the language of authority. We are no longer confident of the virtue or good
will of the people; so it is natural that we fall back on force.
The resort to lawless force—by the Weathermen, the Black
Panthers, the Ku Klux Klan, the hardhats; by the police in
Chicago; by the National Guard at Orangeburg, South
Carolina, and Kent, Ohio; or by highway police at Jackson,
Mississippi—is a confession that both the people and their
government have lost faith in the law, and that the political
and social fabric that has held our society together is un-
raveling: "By such examples," said Lincoln at Springfield,
"the lawless in spirit are encouraged to become lawless in
practice."

It has long been our boast—repeated by the President's Commission on Violence—that notwithstanding our lengthy history of violence we have never had a "revolution," and that our political system appears to be more stable than those of other nations. Our only real revolution took a sectional pattern and was not called revolution but rebellion; since it was rationalized by high-minded rhetoric, led by honorable men, and fought with gallantry, it speedily took on an aura of respectability, and to this day Southerners who would be outraged by the display of the red flag of rebellion proudly wave the Stars and Bars of rebellion.

Thus, like most of our violence, violence against the Constitution and the Union, and by implication against the blacks who were to be kept in slavery, is socially approved. Where such violence has been dramatic (as in lynching or industrial warfare), it has not been widespread or prolonged; where it has been widespread and prolonged (as in slavery and the persistent humiliation of the Negro), it has not been dramatic. Where its victims were desperate, they were not numerous enough or strong enough to revolt; where they were numerous (never strong), they did not *appear* to be desperate, and it was easy to ignore their despair. Now this situation is changing. Lawlessness is more pervasive than ever; the sense of outrage against the malpractices of those in power is more widespread and articulate; and the divisions in society are both deeper and more diverse, and the response to them more intractable.

One explanation of our current malaise is that it seems to belong to the Old World pattern rather than that of the New. Much of the rhetoric of the conflict between generations is that of class or religious wars—class war on the part of, let us say, Vice President [Spiro T.] Agnew; religious protest on the part of Professor Charles Reich and those involved in what he calls "the greening of America." If this is so, it goes far toward explaining some of our current confusion and blundering: the almost convulsive efforts to distract attention from the genuine problems of environment, social injustice, and war, and to fasten it on such phony issues as campus unrest or social permissiveness or pornography. What this implies is ominous: Our society is not prepared, either by history or philosophy, for the kind of lawlessness and violence and alienation that now afflict us.

Why is this so ominous?

Traditionally, our Federal system could and did absorb regionalism and particularism, or channel these into political conduits. More accurately than in any other political system, our representatives represent geographical places—a specific congressional district or a state—and our parties, too, are organized atop and through states. Our system is not designed to absorb or to dissipate such internal animosities as those of class against class, race against race, or generation against generation.

A Concern for Posterity

A people confident of progress, with a social philosophy that assumed that what counted most was children and that took for granted that each new generation would be bigger, stronger, brighter, and better educated than its predecessor, could afford to indulge the young. "Permissiveness" is not an invention of Dr. [Benjamin] Spock [author of the bestselling *Baby and Child Care*] but of the first settlers in America. Today, a people that has lost faith in progress and in the future, and that has lost confidence in the ameliorating influence of education, indulges instead in convulsive counterattacks upon the young.

A nation with, in Jefferson's glowing words, "land enough for our descendants to the thousandth and thousandth generation" could indulge itself in reckless exploitation of that land—the mining of natural resources, the destruction of deer and bison and beavers, of the birds in the skies and the fish in the streams, and could even (this was a risky business from the beginning) afford to ignore its fiduciary obligations to coming generations without exciting dangerous resentment. But a nation of more than 200 million, working through giant corporations and giant governments that ravage, pollute, and destroy on a scale heretofore unimagined, cannot afford such self-indulgence. Nor can it persist in its habit of violating its fiduciary obligations without outraging those who are its legal and moral legatees.

A nation that had more and better land available for its people than any other in history and that, for the first time, equated civilization with the pastoral life and exalted the farmer over the denizen of the city could take urban development in its stride, confident that the city would never get the upper hand, as it were. Modern America seems wholly unable to adapt its institutions or its psychology to massive urbanization, but proceeds instead to the fateful policy of reducing its farm population to a fraction and, at the same time, destroying its cities and turning them into ghettos that are breeding places for crime and violence.

A system that maintained and respected the principle of the superiority of the civil power over that of the military could afford to fight even such great conflicts as the Civil War, the First World War, and the Second World War without danger to its Constitution or its moral character. It cannot absorb the kind of war we are now fighting in Southeast Asia without irreparable damage to its moral values, nor can it exercise power on a world scale without moving the military to the center of power.

No nation could afford slavery, certainly not one that thought itself dedicated to equality and justice. The issue of slavery tore the nation asunder and left wounds still unhealed. Here is our greatest failure: that we destroyed slavery but not racism, promised legal equality but retained a dual citizenship, did away with legal exploitation of a whole race but substituted for it an economic exploitation almost as cruel. And this political and legal failure reflects a deeper psychological and moral failure.

Unlike some of our contemporary politicians, Lincoln was not content with decrying lawlessness. He inquired into its causes and, less perspicaciously, into its cure. In this inquiry, he identified two explanations that illuminated the problem. These—translated into modern vocabulary—are the decline of the sense of fiduciary obligation and the evaporation of political resourcefulness and creativity. Both are still with us.

No one who immerses himself in the writings of the Revolutionary generation—a generation still in command when Lincoln was born—can doubt that the sense of obligation to posterity was pervasive and lively. Recall Tom Paine's plea for independence: " 'Tis not the concern of a day, a year, or an age; *Posterity* are virtually involved in the contest and will be . . . affected to the end of time." Or John Adams's moving letter to his beloved Abigail when he had signed the Declaration of Independence: "Through all the gloom I can see the rays of ravishing light and glory. *Posterity* will triumph in this day's transaction." Or Dr. Benjamin Rush's confession, after his signing, that "I was animated constantly by a belief that I was acting for the benefit of the whole world and of future ages." So were they all.

The decline of the awareness of posterity and of the fiduciary principle is a complex phenomenon not unconnected with the hostility to the young that animates many older Americans today. It is to be explained, in part, by the concept of an equality that had to be vindicated by each individual; in part, by the fragmentation of the Old World concepts of family and community relationships, which was an almost inevitable consequence of the uprooting from the Old World and the transplanting to the New; in part, by the seeming infinity of resources and the seeming advantages of rapid exploitation and rapid aggrandizement; in part, by the weakness of governmental and institutional controls; in part, by the ostentatious potentialities of industry and technology, the advent of which coincided with the emergence of nationalism in the United States; and, in part, by the triumph of private enterprise over public.

However complex the explanation, the fact is simple enough: We have wasted our natural resources more recklessly than has any other people in modern history and are persisting in this waste and destruction even though we are fully aware that our children will pay for our folly and our greed.

Lincoln's second explanation—if it can be called that— was that we had suffered a decline of the creativity and resourcefulness that had been the special distinction of the Founding Fathers. "The field of glory is harvested," he said, "the crop is already appropriated." Other leaders would emerge, no doubt, and would "seek regions hitherto unexplored." At a time when Martin Van Buren was in the White House, to be succeeded by Harrison, Tyler, Polk, Taylor, Fillmore, Pierce, and Buchanan, that expectation doubtless represented the triumph of hope over history. But the decline of political creativity and leadership was not confined to this somewhat dismal period of our history; it has persisted into our own day. We can no more afford it than could Lincoln's generation. At a time when the white population of English America was less than three million, it produced Franklin and Washington, Jefferson and Madison, John Adams and Hamilton, John Jay and James Wilson, George Wythe and John Marshall, and Tom Paine, who emerged, first, in America. We have not done that well since.

Even more arresting is the undeniable fact that this Revolutionary generation produced not only many of our major leaders but all of our major political institutions, among them federalism, the constitutional convention, the Bill of Rights, the effective separation of powers, judicial review, the new colonial system, the political party. It is no exaggeration to say that we have been living on that political capital ever since.

Here again the explanation is obscure. There is the consoling consideration that the Founding Fathers did the job so well that it did not need to be done over; the depressing consideration that American talent has gone, for the past century or so, more into private than into public enterprise; and the sobering consideration that at a time when our chief preoccupation appears to be with extension of power rather than with wise application of resources, those "regions hitherto unexplored" appear to be in the global arena rather than the domestic. Whatever the explanation, lack of leadership is the most prominent feature on our political landscape, and lack of creativity the most striking characteristic of our political life.

It is still true that, "if destruction be our lot, we must ourselves be its author"—that the danger is not from without but from within. But

> ... passions spin the plot;
> We are betrayed by what is
> false within.

For, paradoxically, the danger from within is rooted in and precipitated by foreign adventures that we seem unable either to understand or to control. We have not been attacked from Latin America or from Asia; we have attacked ourselves by our own ventures into these areas.

The problem Lincoln faced in 1838 is with us once again: the breakdown of the social fabric and its overt expression in the breakdown of the law. Lincoln's solution, if greatly oversimplified, is still valid: reverence for the law. A people will revere the law when it is just and is seen to be just. But no matter how many litanies we intone, we will not induce our people to obey laws that those in authority do not themselves obey. The most striking feature of lawlessness in America today is that it is encouraged by public examples. It is no use telling a Mississippi Negro to revere the law that is palpably an instrument of injustice to him and his race. It is no use exhorting the young to obey the

law when most of the major institutions of our society—the
great corporations, the powerful trade unions, the very instruments of government—flout the law whenever it gets in
their way. It is of little use to admonish a young man
about to be drafted to revere the law when he knows that he
is to be an instrument for the violation of international law
on a massive scale by his own government. It is futile to
celebrate the rule of law and the sanctity of life when our
own armies engage in ghoulish "body counts," burn un-
offending villages, and massacre civilians. While governments, corporations, and respectable elements in our society
not only countenance lawlessness and violence but actively
engage in it, violence will spread and lawlessness will flour-
ish. We are betrayed by what is false within.

DEVISING A CURE: TWO GENERAL VIEWS [3]

Fighting crime in America threatens to be handicapped
by a striking difference in emphasis between President
[Richard M.] Nixon, on one hand, and four recent presidential commissions on the other.

The commissions say Yes, the faltering system of criminal
justice in America must be remedied and then they add the
"but"—but unjust social conditions from which crime springs
must be corrected equally.

President Nixon begins from the other end. Yes, he says
in effect, social injustices must be reduced, but poverty is
not the justification for crime. He advocates a tough "law-
and-order" posture.

This difference in approach results in wide differences
on concrete issues, like gun control. A rigorous control law
would reduce "violent crime significantly," said Nicholas
deB. Katzenbach, a former attorney general, who headed

[3] From "The Culprit: Criminal or Climate?" by Richard L. Strout, staff
correspondent. *Christian Science Monitor.* p 17. Je. 5, '71. Reprinted by permission from *The Christian Science Monitor.* © 1971 The Christian Science
Publishing Society. All rights reserved.

the 1967 crime commission under President [Lyndon B.] Johnson. "There is no police official in the country who doesn't know this."

But Attorney General John N. Mitchell argues that the 1968 law restricting imports and interstate shipments must be tested further. Dr. Milton S. Eisenhower's commission on violence reported in 1969, "The deadliness of firearms is perhaps best illustrated by the fact that they are virtually the only weapons used in killing police officers." . . . Mr. Mitchell told the press that he still favors giving the present control act more time before tightening it.

"Lesson Not Lost"

Mr. Nixon's "law and order" posture became a political issue in the 1968 election and again at midterm in 1970. Here are comments by Mr. Nixon:

> Recent [Supreme] Court decisions have tended to weaken the peace forces, as against the criminal forces, in this country.
> The tragic lesson of guilty men walking free from hundreds of courtrooms across this country has not been lost on the criminal community.
> We will reduce crime and violence when we enforce our laws —when we make it less profitable, and a lot more risky, to break our laws. The war on poverty is not a substitute for a war on crime.

When the Commission on Campus Disorders under William W. Scranton, former governor of Pennsylvania, urged use of minimum force, Vice President Spiro T. Agnew denounced it as "pablum for the permissivists."

The Scranton commission was the only one of four of the big "social issue" commissions named by President Nixon. The Katzenbach (crime), Kerner (riots) , and Eisenhower (violence) commissions were all set up by President Johnson, though the latter one (Eisenhower) made its report in December 1969, after Mr. Johnson had left office.

In testimony before a Senate subcommittee here . . . Dr. Milton S. Eisenhower said that a "hard line" for enforcement would not end crime.

He said he favors doubling the amount of money going to the system of US criminal justice (at present around $5 billion annually).

But we must also attack the social causes of crime [he added]. And this, essentially, means not only restructuring the government of our cities but having proper programs in housing, education, employment, commercial opportunities, summer and part-time, and even during-school employment for young people.

The twin attack is absolutely essential.

. . . [Another] commission chairman who testified was Nicholas deB. Katzenbach, former attorney general. "I have great concern," he said, "that we will more and more substitute a billy stick for some intelligent management of law enforcement."

All the witnesses urged big new expenditures as social investment in the war on crime. Dr. Eisenhower's commission recommended $20 billion additional annually. All urged a minimum use of force in meeting crime. They expressed regret that greater use had not been made of their reports.

Dr. Eisenhower's report summed up the feeling: "This nation is entering a period in which people need to be as concerned by the internal dangers to a free society as by any combination of external threats."

SOME DIMENSIONS OF THE PROBLEM [4]

The three sessions of the Congressional Conference on Justice in America were held on Friday morning, Friday afternoon and Saturday morning, May 15 and 16 [1970], in a square, oak-paneled room in the Capitol Building. . . .

As each participant came in and sat down, a staff member of the Fund for New Priorities in America, the sponsor

[4] From " 'Law and Order' 1970," by Ralph Lee Smith, a regular contributor to *The Nation* and author of *The Tarnished Badge. Nation.* 210:774-85. Je. 29, '70. Reprinted by permission.

of the conference, lettered his or her name on a piece of card-
board and propped it up in front of the individual. . . .

The conferees were welcomed by Dr. Arthur Larson,
chairman of the conference, and Representative Claude Pepper [Democrat, Florida] on behalf of the congressional spon-
sors. Senators Philip Hart [Democrat, Michigan] and Harold
Hughes [Democrat, Iowa], who were attending Walter
Reuther's funeral and could not be present, sent statements
which Dr. Larson read. He then offered a few opening comments. . . .

The room remained calm . . . while Senator Sam J. Ervin,
Jr., [Democrat] of North Carolina, led off the discussion with
a description of the District of Columbia Crime Bill, which
provides for preventive detention of suspects under certain
circumstances, and contains a "no-knock" provision, permitting a policeman with a valid arrest warrant to enter or
break into a suspect's home without warning. Senator Ervin
expressed indignant opposition to both provisions. . . .

Jerome H. Skolnick, professor of sociology at Berkeley
and author of *The Politics of Protest* and *Justice Without
Crime,* . . . opened up a second front. "I really don't think
these problems are that easily separable," he said, "but I
would like to address myself to a narrower issue which, I believe, underlies many of Senator Ervin's remarks." The problem, he suggested, is that even if we have the correct laws, the
police are unlikely to observe those that inconvenience them:
"Even if we don't have the no-knock provision, we have the
problem that the police don't knock anyway. That is a very
serious problem because if we are going to conduct this conference on the ground that the rules in fact influence police
behavior, we are going to be conducting the conference on
the basis of a reality that does not exist."

In addition, Skolnick went on, things are made even
more difficult by the fact that the police lie. "The police will
reconstitute facts in such a way as to meet legal standards, by

and large. This is a very serious problem because this leads us to the question ... "

Face flushed, [G. Robert] Blakey [chief counsel of the Subcommittee on Criminal Laws and Procedures of the Senate Committee on the Judiciary] interrupted him. "Nonsense! The truth of the matter is that most of the police, most of the time, live up to the rule, and the problem is with the exception. If we are not going to focus on that kind of problem, that it is the exception and not a general rule that we are worried about, we are right back to the kind of hysteria which will lead this conference to go off in all directions simultaneously."

"May I say," Skolnick replied unhesitatingly, "that the exceptions may be widespread, and it would be very interesting to see how much time police give in general all over the country before they enter, even where you have provisions to the contrary. ... I have never, and I have worked with the vice squad for six months, I have never seen the police give a warning. If they think they have got evidence inside, they knock the door in."

"I have worked with the FBI where we utilize an electronic megaphone and a stop watch, a megaphone to make sure the people on the inside heard, and the stop watch to insure a sufficient amount of time," Blakey retorted. "If the conference is going to leave the people with the idea that your limited experience with one police force in California can be generalized to all law-enforcement agencies, Federal, state and local, it seems to me we are going to perpetuate hysteria."

"I can't allow the assumption that what Professor Skolnick has said can be dismissed either as sampling from one police force or as hysterical, to remain for one moment," asserted Edgar Z. Friedenberg, professor of education in sociology at the State University of New York at Buffalo, and author of *The Vanishing Adolescent* and *Coming of Age in America*. "The report, *Police Power*, for example, which is a carefully documented study and not of a single force either, establishes quite well and simply that the police lie. They lie habitually, continually and as a matter of common sort of standard practice, and they do not do so out of malice."

The reason the police lie, Professor Friedenberg said, is that they feel they have a professional responsibility to see that people do what they are supposed to do. Civil liberties safeguards, "that come from a different class of effete snobs anyway," tend to interfere with proper performance of this professional task. The police feel that their responsibility is to protect society from all the "disorder, misconduct, obscenity and irritation" that would be visited on the populace if nit-picking civil libertarian concepts of procedure were allowed to prevail in dealing with wrongdoers.

There is nothing new in this, Professor Friedenberg continued; the only new thing is that middle-class persons such as students and professors "are now getting the kind of administration of justice that used to be reserved for people too poor and unfamiliar with the process to defend themselves."

Deputy Assistant Attorney General [Henry E.] Petersen joined in. "'To the extent that there is present in this conference a concept that law enforcement is oppressive, I agree," he said. "I would resent it, were I handed a valid search and seizure warrant. I would resent being tried. I do not understand the purpose of due process and law to preclude all oppression, if by oppression is meant trying an individual for a crime he has committed, or arresting a person on a probable cause to believe that a crime has been committed." . . .

The "Non-System" of Justice

The second part of the morning agenda called for a discussion of the nation's law-enforcement machinery. An overview was given by Lloyd N. Cutler, former executive director of the President's Commission on the Causes and Prevention of Violence. The commission, he said, had had many discussions "very much like the first hour of this conference."

In the end [he stated], we concluded that the basic problem was to make violent conduct, that is, illegal violence, both unnecessary and unrewarding.

To make it unnecessary, we felt that the political and social institutions of the country had to be far more adaptable in taking steps to listen to deeply felt grievances and to correct social and political injustice of every kind, including the injustice of many aspects of the law-enforcement system.

As for making illegal violence unrewarding, that turns largely on achieving a better criminal justice system than the one we have today. The criminal justice system is very much underfinanced and very much undermanaged. It is really a misnomer to call it a system at all. In these respects, we felt that it is simply typical of the basic weaknesses of urban government in this country.

He ticked off some features of the "non-system":

The amount that America invests in the criminal justice system—for all police, all courts, all corrections, Federal, state and local—is less than three quarters of 1 percent of the national income, and less than 2 percent of all Federal, state and local tax revenues. That is barely more than we spend on the space program, and less than we spend on agricultural subsidies. Yet "this is the issue that decided the last election, and is going to decide many more elections to come."

"In any city today, the shabbiest, the most overcrowded and the most inefficient public facilities of all are the police stations, the courthouses and the jails." This antiquated setup is now dealing with some 9 million serious crimes per year.

These 9 million crimes produce arrests in only 12 percent of the cases, and conviction in only 6 percent —including a large number of cases in which the defendant agrees to plead guilty to a lesser offense.

"Such a 'system' does not deter, does not detect, does not convict, and does not correct."

The "system" consists of myriad independent entities, each of which tends to blame the others for what goes wrong. There are no common budgets, and in most cities no agency takes a general view of all the components of the system. "It is probably the worst and most poorly managed bureaucracy of all the bureaucracies we have."

Out of the Violence Commission's recommendations, Cutler said, there grew an agency called the Law Enforcement Assistance Administration (LEAA). It was to be a vehicle through which the Federal Government could pump money into local criminal-justice systems on a matching-grant basis. The original plans for LEAA called for $1 billion of Federal funding by the third year of LEAA's existence. In this, its second year, it got only $250 million, of which only $7 million was earmarked for research into all aspects of criminal justice in America.

Is More Money the Answer?

Henry S. Ruth, Jr., director of Mayor Lindsay's Criminal Justice Coordinating Council in New York, pointed out that states and cities are poorly equipped to receive and spend this Federal money. Many state legislatures have been unable to produce the 40 percent of matching funds that the Federal statute requires. Some states have had funds in hand for as much as eight months, and have not spent them because they have no machinery for making the expenditures and no planning mechanisms.

Congress set the $7 million ceiling on the amount that LEAA can spend on research. This is a "disgrace," Ruth said, because at all levels of government there is an "appalling lack of ideas" on how to spend funds so as to bring about real gains.

I think a lot of money already spent has been wasted. You can look at the statistics cited by Mr. Cutler and see that, if we just add a little bit of money for current police, current courts and current corrections, we are not going to be doing anything about the problem at all. We will only aggravate it. . . . We have to get off this platform of shouting for more and more money, and think of ways in which states and cities can be prepared to spend it well.

I would like to see more people talk about the need for alternatives to the criminal process. We just can't keep putting more cases in the courts. The only way the system has survived is by not paying any attention to its ideals. And that is the crisis today.

Representative Claude Pepper, a member of the Committee on Crime of the House of Representatives, said that testimony before his committee had convinced him that there were many viable ideas in the field, and that the urgent issue was more funding. But Wes Pomeroy, former associate administrator of LEAA, sided with Henry Ruth.

We don't know what causes recidivism [he said]. We don't know how to correct people. We don't know how to rehabilitate them. We have a very confused idea about the role of the police, which is very basic and primary and right at the root of the problem.

[Progressive police chiefs, middle management in police forces and patrolmen, he continued] have been waiting for something good to happen for a long time. Now they see a process that is more concerned about who sends out the money and who gets it than what it goes for. They are not getting the leadership out of Washington that they really ought to get.

Some of LEAA's failures, he added, have structural and political origins. The organization is headed, not by an individual but by a troika, an arrangement that "flies in the face of every good administrative principle in the world." Pomeroy was a member of the first troika appointed by President [Lyndon B.] Johnson to run LEAA. The three men worked well together, "but that was just a lucky circumstance, and it may not happen too often again." In addition, the Administration, through Attorney General Ramsey

Clark, gave them wide latitude. "Use your discretion and get the thing going," was the only instruction Clark gave them.

Under President [Richard M.] Nixon and Attorney General Mitchell, however, things have changed. LEAA has been made "an arm of the Administration," and its activities are subject to policy directions with which many in LEAA cannot agree. "It is showing up in the organization," Pomeroy said. "You are having bright guys leave. You have two in this room who have left. And you are going to have more."

Robert L. Emrich, assistant professor and assistant dean of the School of Criminal Justice, John F. Kennedy University, Martinez, California, added another consideration: "If you want to solve a problem, as we want to solve the crime problem, you have to know what the problem is. To know what the problem is and to see whether you are getting results requires one very simple element. You need some data. We literally have no data about crime that are worth much of anything."

What, for example, he asked, is a "serious crime"? By what logic has California tripled the length of sentences for convicted persons over the past ten years? There is no evidence that it has had any effect in reducing recidivism, or any other effect, apart from tripling the cost to California taxpayers.

We have no data on the drug problem, an issue so serious that it has the potential for complete social devastation. There has so far been only one study, poorly financed, on the association between drugs and psychological damage. At the same time, a sampling of Los Angeles physicians over an eighteen-month period showed 2,000 cases of persons seeking such help because of the use of marijuana, and 10,000 cases seeking such help because of the use of LSD. The rate of persons seeking help rose during the period of the study.

LEAA, Emrich said, is heading for the same kind of trouble with Congress that every other domestic program for curing our urban ills has encountered. LEAA will spend large sums; it will have no evidence that the expenditures have lessened the problem; and within a few years Congress will revolt against further expenditure.

The Blacks and the Poor

To the long list of problems, Martha Jenkins, chief counsel of the Lawyers' Committee for Civil Rights Under Law in Cairo, Illinois, and former city attorney of Fayette, Mississippi, added the issues of race and the nation's poor.

In the various state and district law-enforcement agencies and commissions, which decide how the Federal and state matching funds are to be spent, blacks are poorly represented or are not represented at all. The Mississippi State Law Enforcement Agency, with a membership of some twenty to thirty persons, includes one black person—"and that black person happens to be an Uncle Tom." In Illinois, the Land of Lincoln, things are no better. There are no blacks on the local district law-enforcement commission in the area where Mrs. Jenkins works and, in addition, "there is no representation of other significant elements of the community."

"If you want to find out what programs people think might deal with their interests and problems," said Mrs. Jenkins, "then these people have to be represented." At present, "members of the commissions don't have to know various groups in their communities, and don't want to go and find out about them. As a result, most of the money allocated by the districts goes to things like better equipment, shinier badges and guns, new radios and new cars. If the community were allowed to participate in the discussions of what the priorities are to be, I am sure that a lot more constructive ideas would emerge."

Monroe Freedman, professor of law at the National Law Center, George Washington University, and former chairman of the Washington, D.C., Civil Liberties Union, returned to the problem of police perjury and crime.

One group in the society that knows a lot about police crime, but says and does little about it, Professor Freedman stated, is the nation's prosecutors. He cited an article written by a New York University professor who was a former prosecutor, which said that every prosecutor knows police perjury is commonplace.

I brought that quote to the attention of a former prosecutor on my faculty [Freedman said]. He first denied it, and then he said: "Oh, I know, he is talking about perjury regarding technicalities, like unlawful arrest and unlawful searches and seizures."

We know of cases in the District of Columbia, not just perjury cases but police violence cases, that have gone untouched by the prosecution. This is relevant to our concern, not only because police crimes are crimes but also because police criminality breeds criminality. The Riot Commission [Kerner commission] listed four categories of precipitating causes of riots, and these categories were divided into major subcategories. Subcategory No. 1 of category No. 1 was police abuse.

Professor Freedman explained why prosecutors do so little about an abuse about which they know so much:

The prosecutor must depend on the police for his investigation, for his building of the cases, and for his testimony. He must maintain a close working relationship with the police. This is, as I say, a built-in conflict of interest.

I think that any law-enforcement assistance act which does not take this into account is seriously deficient. One of the most important things for us to look toward is an independent arm of the prosecutor's office, or an independent prosecutorial arm, that will police the police without fear of retaliation in the general run of cases that the prosecutor's office has to handle.

At this point the conference adjourned. . . .

Four Important Issues

The theme of the afternoon's discussion was The Effects of "Law and Order" on Justice: Political, Psychological, Sociological Implications. The overview was given by Professor Skolnick, who discussed four major issues:

1. *"Routinized Perjury."* Policemen, he said, have two very different concepts of law. One relates to the substantive law of crimes as committed by members of the populace, and the other to criminal procedure:

> Policemen are much more concerned about substantive criminal law and its violation than they are about criminal procedure and its violation. They regard criminal procedure as a set of obstacles, a set of impediments in their ability to enforce the substantive criminal law. As a result, there are a variety of subterfuges that are used by the police to evade the requirements of due process.

As an example, he cited police testimony in drug cases, as described in a recent article by Martin Mayer. Narcotics users and pushers used to believe that if they were not caught with drugs on their persons, they wouldn't be convicted, so they would throw the envelopes away if policemen approached. The police found this easy to surmount; they would simply testify that they had seen the accused parties throw the envelopes away, whether this was actually true or not. Users and pushers then stopped throwing the envelopes away, thus requiring police to make illegal searches to find evidence. This did not deter the police; they simply made the illegal searches, then continued to testify that they had seen the accused persons throw the evidence away. Judges accustomed to such testimony and agreeing with the policemen's goals, continued to convict. "There are practices that develop within the police department," Skolnick said, "that nasty people would call routinized perjury."

2. *Dissemination by the Police of False and Misleading Ideas About Crime.* Police literature, from FBI materials down through police guild magazines, spreads false ideas about the causes of civic discontent and strife. The Kerner commission, for example, received the following testimony from J. Edgar Hoover on September 16, 1968: "Communists are in the forefront of civil rights, antiwar and student dem-

onstrations, many of which ultimately become disorderly and erupt into violence."

Numerous studies, said Skolnick, refute this theory, yet it is reflected throughout police literature. Therefore, police called in to control a demonstration feel that they face an enemy. They have no true idea of what the protest is about and why it has occurred. They have been indoctrinated in the "rotten-apple" concept, that a few conspiring agitators are causing all the trouble, and that if these persons could be weeded out, peace and bliss would return to the community and the nation.

3. *Drug Policy in America.* The US Government, Skolnick said, "is itself responsible for a majority of crimes in the streets." The illegal status of drugs, in the face of widespread use, forces up the price, creates a criminal traffic, and causes immense numbers of persons to commit crime to get the money for the drugs they want or need.

In the state of California alone, there were fifty thousand arrests for use of marijuana in 1969. The social costs of such laws are enormous. Young people have been told "lies, literally lies" by government sources, about the evil effects of pot. They learn from personal experience that its effects, as nearly as they can tell, are not those described by government propaganda. Actually, "I would say that a kid today on a college campus who hasn't tried marijuana is very uptight. There is something wrong with him, because the peer-group pressure is so great that he cannot fail to try it." The situation is therefore "a fundamental source of alienation of youth."

4. *American Foreign Policy.* "Finally, I would say that the thing that has alienated youth in this country more than anything else is our foreign policy stance. The kids want to know why they have to die for nothing whatsoever. They have to either kill or be killed, and they want to do neither, and they are absolutely powerless." . . .

Justice and the Black Community

Mrs. Martha Jenkins described how law, order and justice relate to one another in Cairo, Illinois, the community in which she runs a civil rights legal office.:

We opened our office there in October 1969. Between March and December of that year a black movement was organized in Cairo.

There were some eighty-six nights of white sniper fire into the black ghetto projects. There was a great deal of violence. The blacks were not able to hold orderly marches. There was no chance for the blacks to participate in government at any level. There are no blacks in the city government. There are no blacks in the fire department. There are no blacks in any positions except janitorial. Local employers don't hire blacks. Rather than hire a black, they will take people from across the bridge in Kentucky.

Cairo is a very poor and incredibly racially polarized town. When we got there, a lot of blacks had been arrested, either for trying to march, or for trying to engage in peaceful, orderly, constitutional modes of expression. A number of blacks had also been arrested on various regular criminal charges, not necessarily because they had committed the crimes but because they were movement leaders.

Our first job was to take care of these criminal defense cases. When we went to the courts, we found that the juries were all white. We stopped trials for a month. The juries do now include, not an adequate number of blacks but at least some.

We tried two criminal cases, and in each of these cases the policeman's story was so preposterous that even with a majority of whites on the juries we won acquittals.

When the establishment of Cairo saw that the black movement people were going to be represented, that someone was going to raise issues on their behalf, that blacks couldn't be talked into copping a plea as they had before, the state's attorney voluntarily dropped something between 70 and 130 criminal prosecutions of blacks.

But the state's attorney, who is the equivalent of the D.A., still refuses to take complaints by black people against white people. If you ask black people to go through the justice system, you are asking them to go to a system to which they have no access and that does not exist to help them.

As for political avenues of change, about a year ago the Illinois House of Representatives sent an investigative committee to Cairo. They made a very good report on racial and economic conditions, and recommended changes to the governor, to the state legislature, and to the local politicians and people who run things. They returned to Cairo, and on May 15 issued a report saying that not one thing had been done about any of their recommendations. . . .

We have taken cases to Federal courts—cases, for example, challenging the all-white makeup of the housing authority, challenging segregated public housing which they admit is segregated, challenging the all-white makeup of several boards and commissions, challenging the lack of due process in the expulsion of black students from schools for behavior for which white students are not expelled or even suspended. We filed these cases back in October.

The Federal judges involved have fine reputations as judges and men. I am sure they are good men, and I am sure they are not doing this on purpose, but I think when they feel there is an unpopular case filed in their docket, the longer they hang it up, the sooner it will go away.

On the cases filed in October, the judge allowed the defendants until January 1 to answer. On January 1, instead of answering they filed a motion to dismiss, on highly technical grounds. The motion to dismiss never got ruled on until May 1, and in the meantime when we tried to make discovery they said No, we don't want any discovery taken until motions to dismiss are filed.

How can you look on these things, politicians, courts, juries, police, as available modes of social change when this is what happens when you try to use them? The black community there is still trying, but I don't know what the answers are. The channels of social change don't work.

I have just one other thing to say, and this is probably the most frightening part. The good people, the people respected in their communities, all over Illinois, they don't listen either. For example, we are trying to raise funds to keep our civil rights law office open, and we talked with the missions committee of one of the major church groups. Their chairman said: "I believe in majority rule, but I believe that once the majority has ruled you just can't let people go into courts and overturn these laws every couple of months, because you are not going to have any respect for law and order and you are not going to have a stable society."

After Mrs. Jenkins' comments, the meeting adjourned briefly. . . .

Justice and the Juvenile Offender

A number of other interesting statements and comments were made during the balance of the afternoon, but perhaps the most impressive was the description by Mrs. Patricia Wald of the problems of certain children in the public school system of the District of Columbia:

I am an attorney with the Neighborhood Legal Service [an organization financed by the Office of Economic Opportunity to provide legal services to the poor]. We do a fair amount of juvenile work. My experience leads me to believe that we are really losing more of the battle every day just in juvenile crime problems than we are winning by whatever progress we are making with the adults here.

Every day you can walk into the District of Columbia schools and you can almost pinpoint large numbers of kids who are really foredoomed or destined to some sort of illegal criminal activity, and most of them don't have a view on Cambodia either, so I cannot attribute it exclusively to that.

We represent many of these kids in school suspension hearings. They first show up with all their problems in the school context, which is the first official society organization they come into contact with.

You can see it written right down there, the fact that the kid is either slightly mentally disturbed, or that there is at least evidence of it. He is acting out. He has had several incidents of violence right within the school. The response is, "Get him out of our schools." Never mind the fact that by suspending him we put him out on the streets; he does not go back to any school because we do not have any facilities to put him in.

There is not a single place in the District of Columbia to which you can refer a juvenile, and no psychiatrist will see him. There is not a single residential treatment facility in the entire District of Columbia for juveniles.

We are really pushing these kids out of society. Very often the same kids we represent in the school suspension hearings, we get back in at the juvenile court door.

The kids we see are profoundly cynical of the system of justice. Very often they try to con us, their lawyers, as much as they attempt to con everybody else. Three fourths of your problem is to get a truthful story out of your client to begin with. They have very little fear of perjury in the courts or anywhere else. I think if I were they, I would feel the same way because it has been my experience that there is not a single helpful thing in the juvenile court system, at least in an urban center like this.

I think research is fine, but I have sat on one crime commission and have been a consultant to three others, and the answers are always the same. After all the research has been conducted, they always say that we need more community facilities, more job-training programs, more special services. The answers, I think, are there, but there is no national commitment to them.

Last week one of the clerks of the juvenile court told me that a boy in a juvenile court cell had slashed his wrists. They were sutured, and he was returned to his cell. He took the stitches out. His wrists were resutured. He took them out again. So they put him into St. Elizabeth's, along with adult psychiatric offenders, in the John Howard Criminal Pavilion.

I think that despite everything we have talked about today, we will continue to lose the battle until we really put our resources and our commitment into the area of the juvenile and really follow through.

Our Overburdened Police

When the conference reconvened on Saturday morning . . . Henry Ruth, director of New York City's Criminal Justice Coordinating Council, scheduled to give the opening "overview" statement, drew a laugh when he prefaced his remarks by saying: "The one dominant thrust of yesterday's session was the camaraderie of outrage!"

Providing some historical perspective, Ruth noted that our system of criminal justice is actually very young:

When the Bill of Rights was written, there were no such things as police departments. There was no such thing as probation or parole until this century. There was no such thing as juvenile courts until this century. On the matter of illegal police procedure, if we look back just forty years, we find that a general method of law enforcement in the cities was for an officer to go down the street and pick out the biggest guy and beat him up and establish his authority on that street.

I think that what has to be done is to look at the police as an organization, and as a group of individuals recruited mainly from a class which hasn't participated in the affluence of America as much as the middle class generally. If we are going to try to do something about police problems, then the community and its political leaders have to tell the police what their role is in society.

At present, said Ruth, the system of criminal justice is performing numerous functions that should properly be performed by other social agencies and facilities, and this is so because these needed agencies and facilities either do not exist or are entirely inadequate:

The police are the only social service agency available from 5 P.M. to 9 A.M. twenty-four hours a day, including Saturday and Sunday. They are finding that up to 80 percent of their time is spent on noncriminal duties, on being a social service agency for the city. The police spend very little time on law enforcement.

The same is true with the court system. The courts are crowded because society has not done enough about its social ills. Instead, it has made these social ills crimes.

I don't think the criminal justice system has ever had a chance, and it never will get a chance until we get these things out of the category of criminal justice and out of the criminal system. I think this is what people ought to be screaming about.

. . . The morning brought a new crop of ideas and controversies, but its highlight was a long, informed comment by former Attorney General Ramsey Clark on the theme of justice in America. . . . It is reproduced . . . [below] in part:

The Law and Moral Leadership

You can't substantially control human conduct in mass, urban, technologically advanced societies through the processes of criminal justice. To think you can is a tragic mistake. Just in the area of more conventional crime, the process of criminal justice doesn't achieve one conviction for every fifty serious crimes under FBI definitions in the United States today. . . .

The best the law can do, the best the system can do, is set some general goals. The law has to provide moral leadership and that is one of these easy phrases. What does it mean? I think we know what it means. I think if the law doesn't say that we stand for justice; that we will pursue it to the extent of our human capacity; if it doesn't provide moral leadership, there is no place that is likely to provide moral leadership.

If the law is to provide moral leadership, the law can't act immorally. The law constantly acts immorally. It acts immorally through what we call over-criminalization, saying we are going to prohibit things we know we can't prohibit. It acts immorally in the very system of due process. Does anyone really think that electronic surveillance isn't immoral? What you are saying is we have to be immoral because we can't protect ourselves any other way.

The same is true of preventive detention, no-knock laws and things like that. But we can't admit that as a society, and we can't practice that. We have to say that somehow or other we can act morally and protect ourselves and survive. If we don't then we are in the jungle. . . .

We are in a real crisis. To me, among the things we have to do is first make the science of institutional change and institutional creation our first order of business. We have got to diffuse power. People have to be able to effect things that are vitally important to them. . . .

We can create new institutions that can bring people some voice in things that are important to them, in the way their garbage is collected, the way their schools are run, the way the police and the courts are conducted. Things like that. . . .

Next, we have to change human attitudes. How do you do that? We have to condition violence from the people's character. It can be done. It has to be done, because we are all up against it. When there are violent people, others will be affected by it.

There are efforts going on now to find out how you go about purging violence, purging racism. . . . We just have to learn to be very introspective and learn as individuals how to purge violence and fear and racism and qualities like this from our being.

I think the young people see this. I think they will tend to change very rapidly. They will have to change very rapidly. I think they can. But the essential thing. you have to work through institutions in mass society because that is the only way that you can make the differences that have to be made. . . . Institutions change today at the leisurely rate of the nineteenth century and that is terribly inadequate.

We can't wait for new leadership in institutions. We don't have that much time. . . .

This is where communication comes in and this is where dissent comes in and this is why, in our time more than any other, the need to hear every point of view is so essential. The principal catalyst in the alchemy of truth has always been dissent. Dissent is a voice of powerless people. If they had power, they wouldn't be dissenting. They would have done. Somebody else would have to dissent.

JUSTICE AT BAY [5]

In all criminal prosecutions, the accused shall enjoy the right to a speedy . . . trial. . . .

The Sixth Amendment to the United States Constitution guarantees this right to all citizens. Like the other nine amendments in the Bill of Rights, the Sixth Amendment was designed to protect one of the most fundamental rights of individuals in a democracy.

Why *is* swift justice so important in a democratic system? Why is a "speedy trial" a basic human right? What happens in a nation where justice is slow?

Four months ago [August 1970] Warren Burger, Chief Justice of the United States, fired an angry barrage of criticism at the American judicial system. Justice in the United States moves much too slowly, he charged. His indictment came in a "state of the judiciary" speech he delivered to a convention of the American Bar Association in St. Louis. [See "Major Steps That Need to Be Taken," in Section V, below.] Burger pictured the US judicial system as a "cracker-barrel corner grocery store" trying to operate in a modern

[5] From "The U.S. Court System Under Fire," by John Starke, staff writer. *Senior Scholastic.* 97:7-10. D. 14, '70. Reprinted by permission of Scholastic Magazines, Inc., from *Senior Scholastic,* © 1970 by Scholastic Magazines, Inc.

"supermarket age." "The judicial process for resolving cases and controversies has remained essentially static for two hundred years," he said.

Such assaults on the judicial system are not new. In 1906 Roscoe Pound (1870-1964), a young Nebraska lawyer who later became dean of Harvard University Law School, lashed out at court delays and what he called the "archaic" system of justice in America. Pound was also speaking at an American Bar Association convention. But most legal authorities at that time attacked his speech as a dangerous threat to the American judicial system. Others agreed with the speech, and were alarmed that Pound's warnings were going unheeded.

Such was not the case with Chief Justice Burger's speech. For more than a decade, American political leaders and legal experts have been referring to delays in the judicial process as the "crisis" in the courts. Some have even claimed the judicial system is near collapse. In 1958 Earl Warren, then Chief Justice, charged that court delays were "corroding the very foundations of government in the United States."

Nearly everyone, regardless of political party or point of view, agrees that the administration of justice is in deep trouble. The problem exists most seriously in heavily populated urban areas. Federal and state courts in most cities are reeling under an avalanche of criminal and civil cases. At the end of June 1969 the eighty-nine Federal district courts in the United States and Puerto Rico had accumulated a backlog of more than 100,000 unresolved civil and criminal cases. And this backlog was growing steadily.

Moreover, the length of time between the beginning of legal action in a case and the resolution of the case is growing longer and longer. Chief Justice Burger reports that "it now takes twice as long as it did ten years ago to dispose of criminal cases." As of last March [1970] 19 percent of the backlog of criminal cases in the Federal courts had been pending for one year or more. Civil cases, on the average, last thirteen months. Some state courts record cases pending for up to four and five years.

Rigor Mortis?

. . . Jury trials often take twice as long now as they did just five years ago. This often poses a hardship for jury members as well as for defendants. There is a standard joke in the legal profession: "This is the only country in the world in which the defendant goes home at night, and the jury is locked up."

Federal courts are also being swamped by appeals from prisoners demanding that their convictions be overturned. In 1961, about 4,000 new cases were scheduled in the eleven Federal courts of appeal. In 1969, the number had jumped to more than 10,000.

With the increase in the volume and length of court cases, already overcrowded courthouses are becoming more and more cramped for space. In the Criminal Court in Brooklyn, New York, some sessions are held in the judges' robing rooms. Before the sessions begin, guards search the closets for defendants who may have escaped.

In 1906, Roscoe Pound spoke of the "paralysis" in the administration of justice in the United States. Today, many believe, "rigor mortis" is setting in. What has caused this breakdown in the courts? Experts cite a variety of reasons:

The US population has soared from 76 million in 1900 to 205 million in 1970. The vast increase has occurred primarily in urban areas, where crime rates are high. Civil suits are also more frequent in overcrowded areas where citizens are more likely to get in each other's way.

A spiraling crime rate accounts for a tremendous increase in the number of criminal cases in state and Federal courts. The Federal Bureau of Investigation reports that the nationwide crime rate last year was almost two and a half times as high as in 1960. In 1969 nearly 2,500 crimes were reported in the United States for every 100,000 people.

Social and technological changes have resulted in an upsurge in certain types of cases and in the addition of completely new *kinds* of cases. As attitudes toward marriage have changed, divorces have become more frequent. More than 25 percent of all US marriages end in the divorce courts. The invention and widespread use of the automobile has resulted in an enormous burden on US courts. In 1965, some three quarters of all civil court cases involved damages arising from auto accidents. Medical malpractice suits and consumer actions against merchants or manufacturers of defective products were almost unheard of a century ago. Today they abound.

In recent decades, Americans have witnessed what some call a "law explosion." Sudden awareness of social ills in the United States gave rise to many new civil-rights laws, voting regulations, and so on. . . . Recent laws pertaining to narcotics have added thousands of new cases.

In recent years, the Supreme Court and Congress have granted more and more protections to persons accused of crime. In 1963, for example, the Court ruled states are required to provide lawyers free for defendants who cannot afford to hire them *(Gideon v. Wainwright)*. That same year, in *Fay v. Noia,* the Court ruled that Federal courts may release state prisoners if police or courts have failed to follow required criminal procedures. Such rulings account for numerous appeals and petitions in Federal courts by prisoners claiming their rights were violated and demanding release or new trials.

Many believe that certain safeguards for the rights of the accused also encourage trial delay. Chief Justice Burger claimed in a 1967 speech at Ripon College (Wisconsin) that some safeguards permit the accused to "use every device of pretrial motions, demands for a new lawyer, and whatnot to delay the moment of truth of the trial day."

The Long Wait

Most people agree that the basic right of Americans to a "speedy trial" *is* in danger. Under American law *all* defendants are presumed innocent until proven guilty. Yet defendants must often wait anxious months or years before their trials begin. In many cases, if they can't afford bail, they are sent to prisons, which are becoming increasingly overcrowded. In New York City, for example, there are about 18,000 prisoners in the various jails. Some 8,000 of these are awaiting trial. People involved in civil cases are often outraged by delays in divorce settlements and other suits. Families are often "pushed to the brink of financial ruin," the *Congressional Quarterly* reports, because months and even years elapse between the time of an auto accident and the eventual court decision awarding damages to pay hospital expenses and auto repair bills.

But these are not the only people who suffer when justice is delayed. Many believe that the rising crime rate—a threat to every American—is partly a result of the failure of law to deter crime. Writes former United States Attorney General Ramsey Clark in his book *Crime in America,* published last month: "A speedy trial is essential if a relationship between wrongful conduct and correctional effort is to be felt." [For additional excerpts from Clark's book, see "Innocence Presumed or Innocence Denied?" in Section III, below.] Chief Justice Burger predicts that trying criminal cases within sixty days after indictment "would sharply reduce the crime rate."

To help combat the increase in crime, Congress recently passed some tough anticrime measures. The new District of Columbia crime control law, signed by President [Richard M.] Nixon last summer, enables judges to keep "potentially dangerous" people in jail for up to sixty days without trial.

It also permits police, in some cases, to enter homes without knocking to search the premises or make arrests. Many believe that such measures jeopardize the freedom and rights of all Americans. President Nixon himself has said that these measures are "strong." But along with most members of Congress, he felt they were essential to protect the public against crime. In any event, most experts believe the measures would not be necessary if justice in the courts were swift enough to deter crime.

II. CRISIS IN THE COURTS

EDITOR'S INTRODUCTION

Drab, scruffy places filled with frightened and bewildered people—that description fits most big-city courthouses today. Even in their physical appearance, our courts
are showing the wear and tear of the mounting strains placed
upon them. And what goes on inside certainly seems in
keeping with their physical condition. The three articles
in this section throw open the doors of the nation's courtrooms to expose the trials and tribulations within.

In the first, an associate editor of *Fortune* tells why many
judges themselves—among them the nation's most eminent
—are appalled by what is happening and, in the light of past
efforts, despair of reform. "The ordinary American," observes
Jeremy Main, ". . . tends to think selfishly that only society's
misfits suffer when the courts fail. But every American is
threatened when justice is threatened." It follows logically
that every American has a stake in redeeming the courts
and making them work. One of the reforms suggested is the
removal from court jurisdiction of "victimless crimes" such
as drunkenness and gambling and also of certain civil matters
such as wills and divorce.

Just how big a problem that may prove to be is fully
documented in the second article in this section. After examining in detail how justice really works—or, more exactly,
fails to work—in the lower criminal courts of the nation,
Richard M. Pious of Columbia University concludes that
the present system "forces judges, prosecutors and defense
attorneys, no matter how interested they are in justice, to
engage in practices which provide neither speedy trials nor
justice. At best only a rough equity is provided," he says,

"and that at the cost of the deterrent power of the criminal code."

The word Pious uses to describe this nonsystem of justice —*dehumanization*—is called to mind in a slightly different context by the final contribution in this section, which recounts the bizarre antics of some lawyers, defendants, and even judges, as political militants try to turn proceedings into an ideological confrontation remote from the immediate issue of innocence or guilt. The author, Louis Nizer, a noted trial lawyer, makes five suggestions designed to restore proper decorum to the halls of justice without, he argues, infringing on the basic rights of the accused.

JUSTICE ON THE VERGE OF COLLAPSE [1]

The machinery of American justice is collapsing. Unless it is repaired quickly and thoroughly, the rule of law itself may disappear. These thoughts are not those of alarmists but of sober, distinguished men of law, such as former Chief Justice Earl Warren and Professor Charles Alan Wright of the University of Texas. One leading expert on court problems, Professor Maurice Rosenberg of Columbia, who contributed in 1965 to a book called *The Courts, the Public, and the Law Explosion*, says today, "My views have changed since 1965 to the extent that what we called a law explosion then looks like a pop by comparison with what we have now." The [former] president of the American Bar Association, Bernard Segal, says, "The danger signals are flashing all over the country, in more places and more persistently than ever."

Megalopolitan, mass-producing society is crushing a court system designed for simpler times. Crime rates are soaring. ... The volume and complexity of litigation today are overwhelming the courts. As Americans crowd together in growing prosperity, they grow increasingly litigious. Suits arising

[1] From "Only Radical Reform Can Save the Courts," by Jeremy Main, associate editor. *Fortune*. 82:110-14+. Ag. '70. Reprinted from the August 1970 issue of Fortune Magazine by special permission; © 1970 Time Inc.

out of auto accidents alone contribute as much as one third of the total work load of some court systems. New products lead to new laws. New social and political forces are taking to the courts. Maddening new elaborations of court procedure sometimes make the search for a true verdict seem irrelevant to the ritual of the trial. In some major court systems, jury trials take twice as long on the average as they did in the mid-sixties.

It is true that American justice has made noble advances recently in terms of protecting the rights of defendants and of providing legal representation to the poor and to minorities. But even these advances are threatened, because the courts just are not working well. To be effective, justice must be both fast and fair. It is the pace of justice that has become distorted. Some courts, usually the lower courts that deal with lesser matters in big cities, race through their case loads on a batch or assembly-line basis so that the whole process become a farce. Other courts, especially big-city trial courts, fall years behind in their calendars. When a citizen has to wait two and a half to five years to be awarded damages, as he does in most large American cities in cases that go before a jury, the wait itself becomes an injustice.

Earl Warren recently recalled that shortly before he left office felony cases in the United States District Court for the Eastern District of New York were taking twenty-two months to get to trial. Because of reforms in the bail system, the accused were free during the wait. However, said Warren, "if the defendant were innocent, think of the cloud over his life, and if he were guilty, think what he could do in those years to disrupt society. This was an atrocious situation that could not under any circumstances be justified."

Today, traveling through a time of exceptional stress, the United States needs more than ever to be escorted by effective justice and by serene, civilized courts. Even in the best of times, American courts have suffered too much from politics, corruption, and judicial incompetence. The legal process seemed too often to be a weapon used by the dominant forces in society against the poor and the minorities, who needed protection the most. The civil-rights victories of recent decades, however, opened the courts to a whole range of new issues and claims. Now the poor and the black are beginning to get the same chance to redress wrongs that other citizens have always had. Major social and political conflicts over the war, youth, and race are going to the courts, and so are new issues such as consumer and environmental claims. Whether the courts can cope with these strains sometimes seems questionable, as was demonstrated in Chicago by the undignified irascibility of Judge Julius Hoffman and the antics of the men on trial before him. "The social conflicts of the times are capsulized in the Chicago Seven trial, and as so often happens, the courts didn't measure up," says Glenn Winters, the executive director of the American Judicature Society.

"The crisis in the courts" . . . has been developing for years. The response to this crisis, led in the last two decades by Warren and former Associate Justice Tom C. Clark, was to try to cure the problem mainly by reorganizing the courts through administrative reform. During the 1950s and 1960s, eleven states followed the example set by New Jersey in 1948 of establishing a unified state court system under the general supervision of the state supreme court. Federal and state courts have tried many kinds of reform in court procedures to shave a few minutes here and there from trial time: split trials, smaller juries, pretrial conferences, "short-cause" trials, and so forth. These experiments in administrative reform on the whole have been disappointing.

There Shouldn't Be a Law

Lately a number of American jurists, more impressive for their prestige and insight than for their numbers, have come to believe a more radical kind of reform is necessary. They think the old refrain, "There oughta be a law," has too often been the nation's approach to solving, or illusion of solving, too many kinds of problems. The criminal courts are used to punish too many crimes that in fact are offenses only against taste and standards of moral or sexual conduct. Shoving drunks, addicts, gamblers, and prostitutes through a revolving-door court process does little to help society or the offenders. The civil courts are imposed upon massively to transact routine business in which there is no real dispute and no doubt about the outcome, or which could be handled more effectively and economically by another process. The courts cannot continue to deal with an exponentially increasing amount of regular business and have society's new problems dumped on them as well. Society will have to choose priorities, and decide anew which kinds of problems are worth the time of the courts and can be solved only by the courts. For the problems that don't pass that test, society should seek other solutions.

Earl Warren and his successor as Chief Justice, Warren Burger, reflect in their philosophies the difference between the old and the new attitudes toward reform. Warren believes that the problem lies not with the law itself, but with how the courts are administered. Burger's concept of the problem embraces far more than administration. For instance, before his appointment to the Supreme Court, he had questioned publicly whether the Fifth Amendment's protection against self-incrimination should be maintained. Again, in a debate three years ago at the Center for the Study of Democratic Institutions at Santa Barbara, Burger suggested that "the adversary process is not the best system of criminal justice." There is nothing in the whole range of law that the radical reformers will not reexamine.

Radical reform of the courts has enormous implications for society because it entails revising our ideas of what constitutes crime, what constitutes conflict, and how conflict should be resolved. Political decisions loaded with controversy, such as whether or not to legalize gambling, would arise. Civil and criminal codes would have to be revised, and constitutional amendments might be needed. Change of

this magnitude, of course, would require new institutions—
magisterial offices and arbitration boards, for example—to
handle matters removed from the courts.

Moreover, the reforms will be difficult to achieve because
the supporters are few if distinguished, the enemies are
numerous, and the apathetic are legion. Lawyers generally
line up with the enemies of reform, because some changes
would eliminate whole branches of law practice. Like the
public, politicians are apathetic because there are no votes
in court reform, and they stand to lose the privileges of
patronage that court appointments offer.

However, interviews conducted by *Fortune* in the preparation of this article indicated a surprising strength of
feeling in favor of a new approach to reform among the
leaders of legal thought, the judges, the law professors, and
some distinguished lawyers.

Eliminating the First Contact

Judges lose their judicial cool when they talk about the
time they must spend on . . . minor crimes. The chief judge
of one of the nation's major city courts protests that dealing
with bookmakers as felons is "a lot of crap." Another big-city
judge, complaining of the time and money lavished on the
case of a vendor caught peddling without a $5 license in a
baseball stadium, said, "We get a lot of garbage that shouldn't
be here."

Dorothy Nelson, the attractive, enthusiastic dean of the
University of Southern California Law Center, sees another
reason for removing certain kinds of cases from the courts.
"We ought to keep people out of the legal system whenever
we can, because once you are in it, it has a lifelong effect.
Sometimes society would benefit if juvenile offenders were
simply allowed to go home under supervision, because even
the best institutions seem to do them harm." The removal
of some sumptuary crimes [i.e. socially offensive conduct
such as public drunkenness] from the law books would in

many instances of minor offenses eliminate this first and
lasting contact with the law.

As in criminal law, in civil law there are matters that
could be "delegalized"—the bookkeeping, form-filling routine
matters which could be handled just as well by a clerk, ac-
countant, or referee as by a judge.

A list of the criminal and civil matters that clearly could
be removed from the various courts includes:

Drunkenness. One third of all the persons arrested in
the United States are charged with no other crime than
being drunk. This has no noticeable effect on alcoholism,
but it has a great effect on the burdens of the courts.

Prostitution. Parading prostitutes through the courts,
often the same ones over and over again, has no uplifting
effect on anybody.

Addiction. The use of drugs, or, legally speaking, the
purchase or possession of drugs, should be decriminalized.
Drug use is imposing a fast-growing burden on the courts,
but treating it as a crime is pointless, although trafficking
in drugs should remain a crime.

Gambling. Betting has become such a part of national
life that few people seriously consider it a crime, including
the policemen who haul in the small fry and the judges
who give them minimal sentences. More than three quarters of the suspects charged with gambling felonies in
New York City last year had their charges reduced to
misdemeanors.

Wills. Probate could be handled by a tax office. Judge
Samuel Silverman, of the New York Surrogate's Court,
says, "Nine hundred and ninety-nine out of one thousand
wills are perfectly all right. So why not just file the things,
the way you do the deed for the sale or transfer of prop-
erty? Why do you have to treat a will as though it were
a lawsuit?"

Divorce. Uncontested divorce is a routine process that
does not require the skill of a judge, yet judges have to

go through the ritual of making it a trial. These divorces
—and nine out of ten divorces are uncontested—could be
handled by an arbiter.

Bankruptcy. Ninety percent of the 200,000 bankrupt-
cies filed in Federal courts are "no-asset" cases, yet the
judges have to go through the whole routine of a trial,
and appoint trustees whose job it would be to distribute
the bankrupt's assets if he had any.

No-Fault for Autos

All these reforms would be overshadowed if the courts
were relieved of their single greatest burden: the automobile.
Along with pollution and death on the highway, the automobile brings us court congestion. Personal-injury cases
flood the trial courts, and traffic cases flood the criminal
courts. "Automobile Accident Litigation," a survey prepared
by the Federal Judicial Center for the Department of Trans-
portation, estimates that 17 percent of all the judge time
in the United States is spent on personal-injury cases arising
out of auto accidents. The more dense the population, the
greater the percentage of auto litigation becomes. In Los
Angeles the superior-court judges spend about one quarter
of their time on auto-injury cases, and New Jersey's trial
judges about one third.

A plan to remove the bulk of auto-injury suits from the
courts has been waiting in the wings since it was first developed at Columbia University in 1932. It would work
something like health insurance or workmen's compensation. The victim would simply collect the damages from
his own insurance company. He would not go to court,
except in special cases. This is "no-fault" insurance; under
the present insurance system, a victim must prove the fault
of another person to collect damages.

In the end the various argument about the legal advantages and disadvantages of the two systems, and their
effects on the courts, will matter little. The issue will be

settled one way or the other by economic interests. The issue lies between the insured, who pay a steep price for unsatisfactory insurance, and the law profession, which exists largely off the proceeds of the insurance. The Federal Judicial Center study estimates that as a result of 220,000 suits arising from auto accidents in 1968, the victims collected a net of $700 million and the law profession (representing both plaintiffs and defendants) collected $600 million plus expenses. The victims who suffer the most collect relatively the least: those with losses over $25,000 collected an average of only one quarter of their losses, according to another Federal study. But the lawyers do well. The most prestigious big-city law firms handle little personal-injury work, or scorn it altogether, but it is the bread and butter of smaller firms and especially of the small-town lawyer. The Judicial Center study estimates that lawyers' contingency fees average 35.5 percent of the recoveries they win for their clients.

[Former] ABA [American Bar Association] President Segal, an energetic agitator for court reform, supports no-fault insurance. "It's inevitable," he says, and he hopes the membership of the ABA will swing around to his view—"We're a little better than the American Medical Association." Right now, however, major segments of the bar vehemently oppose no-fault insurance and have successfully blocked the reform in . . . eight state legislatures. . . .

Reformers also want to move traffic cases, at least the minor ones, those to which automatic guilty pleas usually are entered, out of the courts and into administrative offices, preferably the same ones that handle licenses, so as to make a quick connection between infractions and the suspension or nonrenewal of licenses.

The New York State legislature voted this type of reform last year, relieving the criminal courts of an enormous burden as of . . . July 1 [1970]. Of 5,065,536 cases filed in New York City criminal courts in 1969, 4,600,190 were traffic cases. The majority of these were minor infractions settled by mail, but nevertheless, nearly half of the 150,000 cases pending in June were traffic offenses. On July 1 the New York State Department of Motor Vehicles took over all but the most serious moving violations and a new Parking Violations Bureau began handling parking tickets. The change frees eight criminal-court judges for more important work. Traffic offenders who would have appeared before a judge in court previously now appear in the Motor Vehicles Department before a hearing officer who can impose fines and suspend licenses. There is an appeals board in the department, and defendants can also appeal to the regular courts.

An Invitation to Dry Out

The Vera Institute of Justice, a private organization in New York that experiments with reforms in the area of criminal justice, has organized another kind of alternative to the courts. The Manhattan Bowery Project is an attempt to do something more constructive with alcoholic derelicts than arrest them, take them to court, and give them a suspended sentence. Project rescue teams, consisting of a policeman and a reformed alcoholic, patrol New York's Bowery inviting derelicts to a rescue home, a drying-out "tank" with full-time medical services.

Some offenses could be "decriminalized" without creating a need for substitute ways of handling them. For instance, gambling might simply be let alone. Prostitutes might be allowed to operate—not illegally and flagrantly as they do now, but legally and unobtrusively as they have been doing in parts of Europe for years. For the most part, however, the courts could not be rid of their responsibilities until alternatives had been developed, such as treatment centers for alcoholics, referees for uncontested divorces, and tax offices for wills. The best approach to radical reform of justice might be first to test and develop the alternatives. . . .

Efficiency Is Fictional

Many administrative reforms have come since 1906 when a young lawyer named Roscoe Pound, later dean of the Harvard Law School, first raised the alarm about delay in the courts in a landmark speech. The American Judicature Society was established in 1913 in Chicago "to promote the efficient administration of justice" and the Institute of Judicial Administration was established at New York University in 1948 for similar purposes. Reform of the Federal courts began in the 1930s with the formation of the Administrative Office of the United States Courts. In 1948, New Jersey remodeled its court system along the hierarchical, unified lines laid down by its chief justice, Arthur Vanderbilt, and that set the pattern for a wave of state court reforms.

However, to suggest that these reforms have actually created efficiency in the courts would be pure fiction. In New Jersey, the pioneer, the chief justice theoretically presides over the state's judicial system, but the only people he can appoint are his stenographer, his law clerk, and the court administrator. The governor appoints judges and prosecutors, the sheriffs and the clerks are elected, the municipal judges are appointed by the towns, the probation officers by the courts, and the wardens by the freeholders. No one holds the strings of power, certainly not the chief justice.

Just how badly a court can be run in 1970 immediately strikes even the layman casually visiting the Manhattan division of the New York Criminal Courts. The court is a large, littered building downtown at 100 Centre Street, swarming with bewildered defendants and their families, bored prostitutes, tired policemen, sullen clerks, disheveled Legal Aid lawyers, and harassed judges. Up on the second floor, in the arraignment "part," Judge Irving Lang, a forty-one-year-old former narcotics commissioner, rushes from the courtroom into his robing room, pulls a cigarette from under his gown as he comes through the door, and says, "Welcome to the busiest court in the world." The small, grimy robing room contains a battered wooden desk and a couple of chairs. Sometimes the case load gets so heavy these little robing rooms are used as courtrooms.

During a brief break in arraigning the hundreds of prisoners arrested during night, Lang says he is finishing his third month on the arraignment part and he's exhausted. The normal tour of duty in this courtroom is only one month. Two to three hundred prisoners a day come before him and Lang once arraigned 416 persons between 10:00 A.M. and 5:00 P.M., an average of one a minute even had there been no breaks, which there were. Lang, a conscientious judge, doesn't like it. "It's difficult to be dignified in a situation like this," he says. But the criminal case load is rising by 20 percent a year in New York City.

"Record keeping in this court has broken down completely," says Judge Lang. "All the records show is a man's arrest. If he comes back before us we can't tell, for instance, whether he was out on conditional release or what." Lester Goodchild, administrator of the New York Criminal Courts, wants to install a computer system that would, among other things, easily clean up the backlog in record keeping. But he has no money to do it.

The real scandal is that with all the crush of business, New York City's criminal-court judges spend half their time, according to one survey, waiting for work. The judges are available, but the system that should feed the cases through from arraignment to trial just breaks down. The adjournment is the curse of the overburdened court. The ordinary misdemeanor case in New York Criminal Court is adjourned an average of either four or five times, according to different surveys. The absence of a key figure is the usual reason. Overworked prison officers fail to get the defendant to court, the arresting officer didn't know his case was coming up or else wandered off in disgust after waiting for hours, or an attorney trying to juggle half a dozen cases is tied up in another "part." By the time the fourth or fifth adjournment comes around the case goes stale and justice breaks down.

Too Much "Habeasing Around"

The Superior Court in Los Angeles is better run and more dignified than the New York courts, but it has the same big-city problems. Court filings are increasing five times as fast as the population. At the lower level of misdemeanors the number of guilty pleas has grown, but only because hard-pressed district attorneys and judges are relying more on the great escape valve of the overcrowded court—the reduced charge followed by a guilty plea. That ends the case quickly. If a D.A. tries to make a felony charge stick, a defendant is less likely to plead guilty today because the Supreme Court has given him new weapons of defense to fight with in court. The number of felony trials in Los Angeles increased by 100 percent from 1964 to 1968. And the length of the average jury trial in Los Angeles increased from 3.5 to 7.2 days in the same period. The number of judges in Los Angeles county is rising slowly—from 102 in 1960 to 134 today—but the average case load per judge has soared. The backlog of civil and criminal cases has reached 42,000 and is growing by two hundred a month.

The same sort of conditions exist in many big cities. The Pennsylvania Supreme Court recently stepped in to take supervisory charge of the Philadelphia courts, where enormous backlogs had built up, including 487 untried homicides. In its annual survey of the calendars of state trial courts, the Institute of Judicial Administration reported the average personal injury case took 22.1 months to reach jury trial in 1969, an increase of 1.4 months over 1968 and of 2.2 months over 1966.

Federal courts are also being swamped, especially by post-conviction habeas corpus appeals from state and Federal prisoners who want their convictions set aside on the grounds that their trial violated rights subsequently set forth by the Supreme Court. Most of these appeals have no merit at all, but all this "habeasing around," as one Federal judge puts it, "has crippled the courts." Appeals pending in US courts rose from 852 in 1968 to 1,234 in 1969.

The results produced by various administrative reforms have sometimes proved disappointing, but there is still much that could be done to make the present court system work better. First comes the need to reduce the growing number of "decision points" that [John P.] Frank complains about in his book, *American Law: The Case for Radical Reform*. Whereas a simple criminal trial might once have had just two decision points, the arraignment and the trial itself, a similar case today might involve three additional decision points, each a small trial of its own, on the questions for instance of suppression of evidence (*Mapp v. Ohio*), the right to counsel (*Gideon v. Wainwright*), and disclosure of evidence (*Brady v. Maryland*). There is no question of circumventing the admirable safeguards the Supreme Court has made available to the defense, but of handling them in an orderly manner. They should not be the pretext for the defense lawyer to play games and spin out the trial endlessly with motion after motion.

Judge Shopping

A simple, common-sense answer came from James M. Carter, a Federal judge in California. In 1964 Judge Carter began giving young, inexperienced lawyers a standard check list so that they could be sure they were doing all they should to defend their clients. Four years ago Judge Carter turned this list into a form that, essentially, requires the prosecution and defense to state their intentions at one omnibus hearing held early in a case. If, for instance, the defense lawyer plans to plead insanity, he must say so at the omnibus hearing rather than spring the news at the opening of the trial, which might then be adjourned for weeks while a psychiatrist examined the defendant. The prosecution has similar obligations, especially with reference to the evidence it plans to

present. Judge Carter says the omnibus hearings have short-
ened trials and cut postconviction appeals and motions.

A second promising kind of administrative reform aims to
give judges control of their own calendars, so they can keep
cases moving. Historically the American judge has been a
passive umpire who merely presided over a game played
between contending lawyers. As the courts grew bigger hap-
hazardly, a judge's power to control the progress of a case
was further weakened. Expanding courts proliferated with
specialized "parts," for arraignments, for the calendar, for
motions, for hearings, for different kinds of trials. As a case
progresses, or rather meanders, it moves from part to part
and judge to judge. Lawyers can make endless motions,
use the same excuse repeatedly, go "judge shopping." In
the United States District Court for the Southern District of
New York as many as seven different judges have been involved in one case.

The solution most favored today is known as the individual calendar, which in a sense permits a return to the ways
of a one-judge court in the old days. As soon as possible after
an arraignment or the filing of a case, the matter is turned
over to one judge to oversee for all purposes from then on.
No case wanders from part to part, and the judge in charge
can become knowledgeable about the cases before him and
keep them moving. When the criminal judges in Washington,
D.C., switched last year to the individual calendar they cut
the backlog by 304 cases in three months.

Experts in court reform tend to get carried away by parti-
sanship for the particular kind of calendar system they support. Opponents of the individual calendar, for instance,
argue that in city court systems as big as those of Chicago
and Los Angeles there are just too many judges and too many
cases for the individual calendar to succeed. These courts use
a master calendar. But there are still ways to make sure the
judge gets his hooks in a case. For instance, the specialized
parts in a big court system can be replaced by all-purpose
parts, each of which can handle all phases of a case. All-

purpose parts have been tested successfully in the Queens and Bronx divisions of the New York Criminal Courts and will be used city-wide if and when funds are available.

To run a large court with an enormous turnover competently requires a degree of administrative skill beyond most judges. Many kinds of administrative and management jobs are being turned over to court administrators or executives. They may be trained in law, but it is more important they have a knowledge of business management or systems analysis. At first judges tended to fear administrators or treat them as glorified clerks, but they are realizing that administrators can help make the courts run well without stealing any judicial prerogatives. Some administrators are key men in their courts. Frank Zolin, thirty-seven, an expert in budgets and systems analysis, has nearly the prestige of a judge as the $32,000-a-year administrator of the Los Angeles Superior Courts. His office is next to that of the chief judge. . . .

The thrust of reforms like the omnibus hearing, improved calendar control, and the employment of court executives may have far-reaching effects on the nature of the American trial. While the judge is letting go of administrative functions, he is tightening his grip on what happens in the courtroom itself. He becomes less of a passive umpire in a game between lawyers and more like the European judge who takes charge of the case. The adversary system that Chief Justice Burger questioned three years ago at Santa Barbara becomes modified. He said then that "the [adversary] system is certainly inefficient and wasteful" and "puts all the emphasis on techniques, devices, and mechanisms." With the judge really in charge, controlling the games lawyers play, then the emphasis lies on the truth of the matter before the court rather than the devices and mechanisms.

The Ten O'Clock Judge

The quality of justice depends, in the end, on the judges. Some reformers claim that if only there were enough judges, the other problems of the courts would resolve themselves.

But even if the legislatures were to add large numbers of judges, which is most unlikely, the judges could only overwhelm the problems rather than try to solve them. The real question is the quality of judges. In an introduction to a new book by Professor Delmar Karlen, director of the Institute of Judicial Administration, Burger writes almost longingly of British justice, particularly of the caliber of British judges and lawyers. He notes that with far fewer judges and lawyers per capita than the United States (New York City alone has almost as many judges as there are in all of England), British justice manages to be swift, dignified, and fair.

The United States has produced its share of great judges, especially at the Federal level, but the run-of-the-mill judges are too frequently incompetent, especially at the state and local level. And the corrupt judge is almost as familiar as the corrupt policeman. Methods of appointing and electing judges, being so ripe with political plums, tend to resist reform. However, there is some progress. Eighteen states now use some version of the Missouri plan, which provides for nonpartisan boards of lawyers and laymen to draw up a slate of candidates from which the governor selects his choice to fill a vacancy on the bench. The Missouri plan bases selection on merit rather than politics.

Judicial pay is improving, as are the standards required of judges both through revised codes of ethics and through the bar's scrutiny of candidates for the bench. Judicial education is improving slowly. The United States is the only Western country where law school offers no specific training for the bench; however, in 1956, the Institute of Judicial Administration established an appellate judges' seminar. Other regular seminars have been established since, and in Reno there is a school for state trial judges.

"Qualifications commissions"—watchdog groups of lawyers and laymen that have been set up in seventeen states—have developed recently into the best device for improving performance on the bench. They have the advantages of

plaint rather than observation by a police officer, investigation may result in charges being dropped. The prosecutor also determines whether the police acted legally in making the arrest, especially if a search or a seizure was involved. He may drop the case if evidence was improperly obtained. The prosecutor attempts to gain admission of certain facts and a confession from the accused.

In less serious misdemeanors, especially those in which the police officer is the only witness, arrest of the defendant may not be desirable. For one thing, the drain on police manpower in taking the defendant to the police station, then to a detention facility, and finally to a magistrate is considerable. Some jurisdictions are replacing the arrest system with a summons or citation system in which the accused is directed to appear before a magistrate at a particular time. In New York City, for example, in cases of simple assault, petty larceny and malicious mischief, the accused is interviewed at the stationhouse and the precinct desk officer is authorized to release him with a summons. More than 95 percent of those released appear at the scheduled time. (Some of the remainder are in jail for other crimes or are in the armed forces.) The *Federal Rules* authorize such a summons system, but at present it is in regular use only in the United States District for Northern California. State or city systems operate in California, Michigan and Washington, as well as in New York.

At the initial appearance, which usually occurs within hours after an arrest or days after a summons or citation, the magistrate or judge will inform the defendant of his right to counsel, will assign counsel if the defendant requests it, and will set a date for a preliminary hearing. He will also set bail.

The Bail System

Bail is the requirement of a cash bond or collateral from the defendant or the setting of some nonfinancial condition which will ensure that the defendant will return for trial.

The Eighth Amendment states that "excessive bail" cannot be required. Some leading historians of the bail system, such as Caleb Foote, argue that the framers intended to make bail an absolute right for defendants in all cases. But the Federal Judiciary Act of 1789, subsequent Federal legislation and most state legislation exclude capital crimes from the bail system.

In both the Federal and state court systems, the major criterion for release is supposed to be the probability of appearance for the trial. In practice, judges sometimes set bail according to the nature of the offense or the possible danger to the community if a defendant were released. High bail has become a means of preventive detention of defendants before trial. Moreover, civil rights demonstrators and other protestors arrested at demonstrations have sometimes been held in high bail for minor offenses.

Most defendants find it difficult to post the entire amount of a cash bond. Instead, they pay a premium to a bail bondsman, who provides the bond for the court. In practice, the bondsman decides whether or not a defendant will be released. The unpopular defendant may be refused a bond. The poor defendant cannot provide the collateral needed for a bond. The professional criminal, on the other hand, is considered a "good risk" and can often obtain a bond with no collateral.

In many states, the bondsmen have not been regulated. Some are affiliated with organized crime syndicates. Others engage in unethical referrals with lawyers, and some bribe police who will refer clients to them. Premiums are not always regulated, and sometimes are between 10 and 20 percent of the bond set.

Most of the poor are unable to make bail. In New York City in 1966, for example, one fourth of the defendants could not make $500 bail, almost one half could not make $1,500, and almost two thirds could not make $2,500. Defendants who cannot make bail are placed in pretrial detention facilities—in other words, in jail.

The pretrial detention facilities in most states are old (one fourth are over fifty years old) and in dilapidated condition. Most are overcrowded, with no facilities for exercise, recreation or rehabilitation. Visiting hours are short and inconvenient; phone calls are prohibited; and mail is censored. Defendants placed in jail cannot pay anyone else to investigate for them. Families, deprived of the head of the household, also suffer financial and personal hardship. The first offender is placed in contact with repeaters, and may become bitter and disillusioned.

Early in 1971, there were over eighty thousand people being held in state prisons who had not been convicted of any crime. In large cities the time spent in jail waiting for trial could be considerable: in 1971, in New York City, the average length of time was 114 days, and in Philadelphia, 160 days. Two fifths of the inmates in New York City in 1970 waited a year or more for their cases to be tried.

A person detained before trial may find his case prejudiced. In Philadelphia, two groups of defendants were studied: one group had made bail and had been freed, the other had not and had been jailed. Of 529 defendants who made bail, only 275 were convicted of crimes, and only 61 were sentenced to prison—22 percent of those convicted. Of the 417 defendants who could not make bail, 390 were convicted, and 200, or 59 percent of those convicted, received prison sentences. In New York City, a study revealed that 54 percent of those convicted of crimes received suspended sentences if they had been on bail, while only 13 percent of those who had been in pretrial detention received suspended sentences. Little of this disparity could be explained by the difference in the characteristics of the two groups.

Bail Reform

The cash bail system is based on the assumption that if a defendant posts bail he will appear for trial. In 1961, the Vera Foundation, New York University, the Ford Foundation and the New York City criminal courts began to experiment with nonfinancial release conditions. The Manhattan Bail Project permitted the release on recognizance (a promise by the defendant to the court that he will return) in certain categories of offenses after interviews with law students from New York University. The interview established the defendant's ties in the community, which became the criterion for nonfinancial bail conditions. In the first thirty months of the project, 99 percent of those released returned for trial, compared to 97 percent of those released on bail.

Moreover, the release on recognizance affected the disposition of cases. The released group was compared with a control group of defendants eligible for release but instead not released for lack of bail funds. In the group released, three fifths were not convicted, and of the two fifths convicted, only one sixth were sent to prison. In the control group of those eligible for release but actually placed in pretrial detention, less than one fourth were not convicted. Nine out of ten defendants convicted were sent to prison.

The National Conference on Bail and Criminal Justice, sponsored by the United States Department of Justice in May 1964, concluded that the bail system needed reform. In 1966, Congress passed the Bail Reform Act, which authorized Federal judges to release persons charged with involvement in other than capital offenses on a promise to appear for trial, an unsecured bond, the custody of a third person or organization, or on a premium on a bond deposited in the court and refundable upon appearance for trial. The judge could impose nonfinancial conditions on release, including restrictions on travel, abode and associations. All conditions could be quickly appealed in the district and appellate courts.

The Bail Reform Act did little to change the system in practice. Only in the District of Columbia is provision made for a Bail Agency which can advise the judges on conditions they should set for bail. Elsewhere the Federal judges continue to rely on financial conditions. There is no agency to supervise those released on nonfinancial conditions. Few social agencies are prepared to accept defendants in third-person custody, and there is no mechanism for referral. It is doubtful that states will adopt nonfinancial conditions, since additional funds are required in order to make such a situation work. New York City is an exception: the success of the Manhattan Project led to its expansion and the assumption of investigative duties by the Office of Probation.

Preventive Detention

Preventive detention has recently been proposed in Federal and state legislation as a new bail reform. [See "Innocence Presumed or Innocence Denied?" in Section III below and "The Case for Pretrial Detention," in Section IV, for further details.] Such preventive detention would be based on a judgment by a judicial officer that the release of the defendant on bail before trial would constitute a danger to the community. A number of study commissions have endorsed the concept, including the President's Commission on Crime in the District of Columbia (1966), the Judicial Council Committee to Study the Operation of the Bail Reform Act in the District of Columbia (1969), and the President's Commission on the Administration of Justice (1966). However, the Task Force of the Eisenhower Commission on the Causes and Prevention of Violence rejected it in 1970.

Studies have produced conflicting estimates of the percentage of defendants released before trial who commit additional crimes in that period. In 1968, a study by the Department of Justice conducted for four weeks in the District of Columbia indicated that 11 percent of those released were charged with additional felonies or misdemeanors. Two thirds of the latter charges involved misdemeanors, and most occurred at least thirty days after the original charges. Thus, if trials had taken place sooner, many of the later crimes might not have occurred.

President Richard Nixon proposed a preventive detention system for Federal courts on July 11, 1969, with the introduction of S.2600 in the Senate. A similar provision for the District of Columbia, S.2100, was introduced later. These measures would permit a Federal judge to consider the danger to the community in setting nonfinancial conditions for bail, and would also permit him to order a defendant detained for sixty days before trial in certain specified felony cases, or where a defendant was attempting to harm or threatened to harm a juror or witness. These measures were aimed primarily at recidivists. Neither bill was passed in 1969.

In the spring of 1970, the bills were again introduced, and fourteen other preventive detention bills were filed in Congress. In May, hearings were held before the Senate Judiciary Subcommittee on Constitutional Rights. Officials of the Department of Justice testified for preventive detention; in opposition were [Senator] Sam Ervin [Democrat, North Carolina], the subcommittee chairman, and former Attorney General Ramsey Clark. On June 18, the American Bar Association went on record opposing preventive detention, and the following day the proposal was opposed by the American Civil Liberties Union. The measure has not passed in Congress.

Preventive detention has been authorized in the District of Columbia with the passage of the District of Columbia Court Reorganization and Criminal Procedure Act of 1970, signed into law on July 29, 1970. Beginning on February 1, 1971, it authorized preventive detention for up to sixty days, and speedy trials for those detained. In February, two narcotics addicts were detained by a judge even though the Prosecutor's Office had not recommended it. The Prosecutor withdrew a request for preventive detention in a case involving a suspect charged with felonious assault who had been convicted of thirty-seven misdemeanors and who was also facing charges for murder and robbery. A United States magistrate refused to grant pretrial detention in a case involving assault with intent to rape, instead releasing the accused to the District of Columbia Welfare Department with strict bail conditions. Two other prosecutor's requests were also denied by the courts in February. Until the Supreme Court ruled on challenges to the act brought by the American Civil Liberties Union and the Defender's Service of the District of Columbia, it was likely that it would be used sparingly in the District.

Some states are preparing their own preventive detention acts. On March 22, 1971, a bill was introduced in the New York State legislature which would deny bail to those accused of a serious crime if they had been convicted of a similar charge within ten years prior to the arrest, if the judge found that the release posed a danger to the community.

Those who favor preventive detention argue that certain persons, such as drug addicts, are likely to commit crimes while released on bail. Preventive detention is currently authorized in capital cases, and is practiced when high bail is set in other cases. The proponents of the measure argue that it will regularize the procedure, provide for safeguards and review and give priority to those detained in setting trial dates.

Those who oppose preventive detention argue that it might be unconstitutional, since it may violate the Eighth Amendment. In addition, it may be unworkable. There is no way to distinguish between defendants who will commit additional crimes and those who will not. For a judge to make a determination, he would need additional investigative resources. Instead of spending the funds for that purpose, opponents of preventive detention urge that additional judges should be provided to speed up trials. This would limit the possibility that a person released on bail would commit additional crimes. Preventive detention, it is further argued, might prejudice a jury, especially since in the District of Columbia it can only be used if a judge finds "substantial probability" that the person is guilty of the offense charged.

Preventive detention measures could open the door to the repression of free speech, demonstrations and political activity. If "conspiracy" were added to the list of crimes, the measure could keep political activists in jail and prevent the adequate preparation of defenses. One could certainly expect this result in state courts, especially in the South.

Other Steps Leading to Trial

The other proceedings which lead to trial are the preliminary hearing, the grand jury indictment or prosecutor's information in felony cases, and the plea arraignment. The purpose of these proceedings is to permit the defense to discover a reasonable amount of the prosecution case (in return for revealing some of its own case) and to allow the prosecution to convince the court that there are grounds for a trial. The preliminary hearing forces the prosecution to present a *prima facie* case that the defendant is guilty, and if it cannot do so the charges will be dismissed. Ordinarily, the defense presents no evidence of innocence, although the Supreme Court in a series of cases (*Gideon v. Wainright* [372 U.S. 335, 1963], *White v. Maryland* [285 U.S. 262, 1958], *Pointer v. Texas* [7 Wallace 700, 74 U.S., 1869]) gives the defendant the right to have counsel present. The prosecution also uses the hearing to obtain testimony from witnesses while events are fresh in their minds.

In felony cases the next step in the Federal system and in about half the states is the grand jury presentation. The proceedings are held in secret, and witnesses may be offered immunity for testifying, or charged with contempt if they refuse to testify. The prosecutor conducts the proceedings. The grand jury either returns an indictment or, if the evidence is insufficient, dismisses the charges. In states that do not use a grand jury, the prosecutor proceeds after the preliminary hearing by filing an information with the court. In both systems, the defense may waive both the preliminary hearing and the grand jury proceeding in the Federal system and in many states. The defense may wish to do this in order to prevent the prosecution from discovering certain testimony, or finding out if the defendant intends to plead guilty.

The next step is the arraignment. The purpose of this step is to plead not guilty or guilty. If the plea is not guilty a trial date is set; if the latter, a sentencing date is set. The defendant at this time requests or waives a jury.

After the arraignment, the defense will make its pretrial motions, in which it seeks the discovery of certain evidence which the prosecution may possess, or a change of venue, and so forth. These motions lead up to the actual trial, at which guilt or innocence is determined by a judge or by a jury.

Most of these proceedings move slowly, with adjournments of the trial date common. Thus there is ample time for the defendant to commit additional crimes if on bail. For those defendants held in jail, there is time to become disillusioned with the system and brutalized by jail conditions.

Delay is caused primarily by certain defendants. They may want time to arrange private affairs in case of conviction. Delay may be useful if the prosecution relies on witnesses; time may dim their memory or they may be persuaded to change their testimony. Delay may enable the defendant to shop around for a lenient judge. Defense counsel may explain to the judge that "Mr. Green," a key witness, is not present. This is a code phrase which means that the attorney has not been paid by his client. The judge will oblige the attorney by adjourning the case until the defense counsel receives his fee.

The Non-Trial System of Criminal Justice

The increase in crime rates and arrests and the delays caused by defendants produce overcrowded court calendars. The result is that approximately half the arrests result in the dismissal of charges or the dropping of charges, and nine of ten of the remaining cases are disposed of without trial after pleas of guilty. Less than one tenth of those persons charged with crimes ever go to trial.

Prosecutors have a number of reasons for dropping charges. First, the police may have acted improperly in making the arrest or obtaining evidence. The prosecutor may not want to brand a defendant, especially a juvenile or a prominent citizen, as a criminal. Charges are often dropped in domestic disturbances, assaults, petty thefts and shoplifting, joyrides, drunkenness, disorderly conduct and vagrancy.

Plea Bargaining

Nine of ten cases in which charges are not dropped result in guilty pleas to the original or lesser charges. The defendant pleads guilty at the arraignment after his counsel confers with the prosecutor and sometimes with the judge. This process is known as plea bargaining, because the defendant in effect bargains away his right to a trial in return for his guilty plea to a lesser charge, dismissal of counts in his indictment, the promise of probation or a suspended sentence, or the promise of lenient sentencing on the original charge. [For a detailed account of plea bargaining, see "An Insider's View of Justice in the Courts," in Section IV, below.]

For the guilty defendant, there are a number of advantages in bargaining rather than going to trial: usually his time spent in jail before trial will be credited to his sentence, and sometimes he may be released from jail after sentencing without spending any time in a penitentiary. He also avoids counsel costs for trial. If the defendant loses a trial, he may receive a long sentence. Even an innocent defendant is tempted to plead guilty to a lesser charge if he believes he can walk out of jail after sentencing but must remain in jail if he insists on a trial.

Assigned counsel and public defenders encourage guilty clients to engage in plea bargaining. The Public Defender has a large caseload and a small investigative staff at best.

He has little time to investigate the defendant's case and prefers to concentrate on capital crimes or cases in which the defendant claims innocence. The assigned counsel receives little compensation, is usually not a criminal lawyer, and wants to return to his own practice. He will encourage a guilty plea to end the case. Since the assigned counsel or defender systems represent over half the felony defendants and about one third of the misdemeanor defendants, plea bargaining is encouraged in most cases.

The prosecutor also gains advantages. He must prosecute a large caseload, and he has fewer resources than he needs. He prefers to concentrate on the more important felony and capital cases. Moreover, the prosecutors want to present a high conviction rate to the public, and guilty pleas provide that rate with little expenditure of resources.

Plea bargaining provides advantages to the judges as well. New York City provides an illustration of the necessity of plea bargaining. Under ideal circumstances, a judge might dispose of 44 felony cases a year with trials. In Manhattan in 1966, there were only nine judges handling felony cases: they could have tried a maximum of 396 cases. Yet there were 4,614 felony cases in 1966 in Manhattan. An additional 100 judges would have been needed to try these cases, not to mention additional courtrooms and court personnel. Without guilty pleas, the criminal justice process in many parts of the country could not function. Judges realize this and encourage guilty pleas by implementing the agreements reached by prosecutors and defense counsel. Sometimes they actively participate when agreements are made.

Plea bargaining also mitigates the severity of the criminal codes enacted by Congress and the state legislatures. It enables the prosecutors and judges to temper justice with mercy, especially when dealing with first offenders.

Plea bargaining also keeps the costs of operating the court and penal system manageable. It permits the system to operate with fewer judges, less personnel, and fewer courthouses. By releasing people after short terms or after sentencing, it keeps the prison population lower, thus lessening the need for additional penitentiaries and personnel.

However, there are problems associated with plea bargaining. There is no certainty for the defendant, since the practice is unofficial and subject to understandings reached with the prosecution and judges. Sometimes these understandings are interpreted differently by the parties involved. On the other hand, defendants guilty of very serious crimes can plead guilty at times to minor offenses. In a recent case in New York City, a man accused of the attempted rape of a baby received a one-year sentence. Innocent defendants may plead guilty to minor charges in order to gain their release from jail. Plea bargaining breeds disrespect for the statutory penalties for offenses, which weakens the deterrent effect of the law.

A system that depends on plea bargaining rather than on speedy trials is susceptible to breakdown. When police make arrests in demonstrations, charges are sometimes dismissed if the protestors demand their right to a jury trial. Plea bargaining reduces the pressure on police to adhere to constitutional safeguards in making arrests; if cases are not tried, there will be no exclusion of improperly obtained evidence, and the disposition of the defendant will not depend on police behavior in making the arrest.

Improvements in the system have been suggested. The prosecutor and defense could exchange complete information on the case; the prosecutor could publish standards and procedures to standardize the deals he offers; and the judge could preside more effectively over the process.

Another improvement in the system might be noncriminal disposition of cases. Instead of plea bargains, the defendant and prosecutor might agree to a disposition that would remove the defendant from the criminal justice process entirely. This approach has traditionally been used with defendants of draft age; judges will dismiss charges against first offenders if they promise to enlist in the armed forces.

Procedures could be established (as in a New York program) to refer defendants to employment programs, or to social welfare, hospital or other appropriate agencies. Philadelphia is experimenting with a preindictment program in which charges are dropped after a six-month compliance with probation conditions set by a magistrate.

Conclusion: Getting Worse

The system of criminal justice in the lower courts is well on its way to collapse. It provides precious little justice, and tolerates behavior little short of criminal in bail bondsmen. It forces judges, prosecutors and defense attorneys, no matter how interested they are in justice, to engage in practices which provide neither speedy trials nor justice. At best only a rough equity is provided, and that at the cost of the deterrent power of the criminal code.

The crime rate continues to increase, and the professionalization of police forces also continues. Both result in increases in the total number of arrests. Unless the courts revamp their pretrial procedures, the present system will get worse. Defendants will languish in jail for longer periods of time, while some of those freed will commit crimes, thus increasing the pressure for pretrial detention. Plea bargaining, with its attendant problems, will continue to provide the only tolerable means of keeping the system going. The poor, the first offender and the unpopular defendant will continue to suffer the most. Dehumanization of those in the system, as well as those who pretend to ignore it, will continue unabated.

THE COURTROOM AS CIRCUS [3]

In 1944, the United States Government tried thirty American Nazis and Fascists for undermining the morale of our armed forces then at war. Among the defendants were

[3] From "What to Do When the Judge Is Put Up Against the Wall," by Louis Nizer, a noted trial lawyer, author of *My Life in Court*. New York *Times Magazine*. p 30-1+. Ap. 5, '70. © 1970 by The New York Times Company. Reprinted by permission.

Gerhard Wilhelm Kunze, Fritz Kuhn's successor as head of the German-American Bund; Elizabeth Dilling, who had attended Hitler's giant 1938 Nuremberg rally; George Sylvester Viereck, a German agent; William Dudley Pelley, head of the Silver Shirts movement; Joseph E. McWilliams, head of the Christian Mobilizers; Lawrence Dennis, self-styled Nazi, who insisted on defending himself, and others. They had published leaflets hailing Hitler as a savior, and denouncing President [Franklin D.] Roosevelt as a Jew and warmonger. This printed material was being disseminated among American troops by devious means.

The trial took place in Washington, D.C., Justice Edward C. Eicher presiding. From the first moment that the case began, the defendants and their lawyers did not act as participants in a trial, but like storm troopers—spitting abuse at the judge and the judicial system. Some gave the Nazi salute. They kept the courtroom in an uproar.

Every obstructive device was used calculatingly. When a document was offered in evidence, each lawyer read it separately for ten or fifteen minutes. Then he would hand it to his client, who studied it leisurely. Then each of the thirty lawyers, in turn, would rise to make his objection—in as belligerent and insulting a manner as possible, engaging the court in lengthy polemics. The judge attempted to do what is often done in complex trials, such as antitrust suits with twenty or thirty defendants—to stipulate that the lead counsel's objection would protect all, unless one desired to add some special point. But no, that would not do. The prosecutor attempted to avoid the resulting delay by giving documents to each of the counsel in advance. That did no good, either.

Judge Eicher practiced restraint. He had been advised that if he retorted and struck back at counsel or the defendants, he would be playing into their hands because he might create reversible error. So, day after day, he listened patiently to abuse and insults directed at him.

On one occasion, he was provoked to act, and discharged a lawyer named James J. Laughlin who had been particularly abusive. Thereupon, his client, Robert Noble, set up a cry that he would accept none of the defense lawyers whom the judge assigned to him. He insisted that he had been denied his constitutional right to select his own lawyer. His screams prevented testimony from being heard. There was pandemonium in the courtroom. The prosecutor fell upon the device of severing Noble's case from that of the other defendants so that there would be a little peace in the courtroom. The judge granted the motion. So Noble was rewarded for his contumacy by walking out of the courtroom. He was never again brought to trial on this charge. The other defendants, encouraged by this successful maneuver, redoubled their unruliness.

Judge Eicher grew perceptibly weaker each day. At the end of seven months (the case could have been tried in about twenty days), after a particularly unnerving day, he collapsed. That night he died. His death automatically created a mistrial.

There were 18,000 pages in the record, only 1,000 of which contained testimony. The other 17,000 pages were filled with bickering and colloquy among counsel, the prosecutor and the judge. The Government prosecutor, O. John Rogge, decided not to try the case again because he did not know how he could cope with the defendants and their counsel in another such ordeal. So, the defendants walked out of this courtroom free (though some, including Noble, were sentenced in other trials on other charges). Their strategy to paralyze the judicial process had resulted in killing the judge. It had been a brilliant success.

"You Are Wearing Me Down"

A cynic once said that experience is a wonderful thing because it enables us to recognize our error every time we make it again. Let us move on from 1944 to 1949 and the Communist trial before Judge Harold Medina in the Federal

District Court in New York. It is interesting to observe that counsel and defendants in that trial patterned their battle plans precisely after the successful conduct of the defendants in the sedition trial of the Nazis. The same flanking movements of obstruction and procrastination were employed; the same frontal assault upon the judge to wear him down by insolence; the same gathering of batteries to cannonade the courtroom with furor and tumult.

When the witness Herbert A. Philbrick took the stand for the Government to offer in evidence a Communist party card, merely to illustrate that Communists referred to one another by first name only, each lawyer carefully studied the card at length, back and front, and then gave it to his client who did the same, and then turned it over to the next of the eleven defendants and counsel as if there were some great mystery to be unraveled. When Judge Medina protested the delay, they screamed that their constitutional rights were being denied and that he was a Fascist.

When a telephone book was offered to identify a number, the defendants refused to accept it without authentication. An executive of the American Telephone and Telegraph Company was subpoenaed and put upon the stand, and each counsel for the defense proceeded to cross-examine him at length as to his birthplace, his education, his family and the kind of duties he performed at the telephone company. When the judge attempted to put an end to this farce, there were interminable protests and angry colloquies, until he was forced to call a recess.

On one day alone, thirty motions were made by defense counsel. They were picayune—for example, a motion to close the doors during lunch hour. But the resulting arguments lasted almost two days.

At another point, one of the defense lawyers charged Judge Medina with lying "particularly at 11:20 A.M. and 3:20 P.M. in the afternoon." The judge, intrigued by such specificity, asked: "What does the time element mean?" The lawyer said: "That is the deadline for the morning and afternoon editions."

"You have a terrible mind to make an accusation of that kind," Judge Medina replied, "but you will not goad me into making any statements which will create error in this courtroom. But I plead with you, stop it. You are wearing me down. I don't know whether I will be able to last through this trial, but I will do my utmost to do so." He called frequent recesses so that he could lie down in his anteroom to recuperate. At times, sedatives had to be administered.

As the barrage of invective and disobedience went on, the judge resorted to adjourning court at Friday noon, so that he could have a long weekend to recover. The defendants and their counsel feared that the judge might be slipping out of their hands, and—as the record shows—intensified their attacks on Friday mornings. Despite this venom, the judge was inhibited from retorting or defending himself, because to do so might achieve the defendants' purpose— reversible error. In short, our system lacks the common-sense means to deal with judicial sabotage.

Judge Medina, thanks to his vigor, survived. The trial was completed. The defendants were convicted. The judge went away for a long vacation to recover from his ordeal. When he returned, he was a popular hero. Isn't that sad, too? If a judge can last through one of these trials, we hail him as if he were a hero returning from Bataan. In order to preside at one of these trials, must the judge pass a rigorous physical test? If he is a scholar living a sedentary life, must he be disqualified because he won't be able to withstand the strain? Are we helpless to deal with this kind of situation?

The Chicago Seven

In the recent Chicago trial, eight (later reduced to seven) defendants were charged with conspiring to incite a riot, and individually crossing state lines with that intent, during the 1968 Democratic National Convention, and of performing acts to achieve that purpose. They and their counsel not only imitated the tactics of the defendants in the sedition and Communist trials, but raised them to new peaks of audacity.

One of the defendants upbraided Judge Julius J. Hoffman for having a picture of George Washington on the wall behind him, because "George Washington and Benjamin Franklin [were] slave owners." They refused to stand when the judge entered the courtroom. They referred to him insolently as "Julie," "Hitler," "fascist pig," "liar," "sadist" and "executioner," and told him he "will go down in infamy." They screamed obscenities which, even in the most permissive circles, would be considered extreme. They brought a Vietcong flag into the courtroom. They ridiculed the court by putting on judicial robes.

The lawyers did nothing to quiet their clients; indeed, they supported and justified the outbursts. Early in the trial, Judge Hoffman appealed to them to control their clients: "In the circumstances of this case, this situation, sir, you, a lawyer in the United States District Court, permitting your client to stand up in the presence of the jury and disrupt these proceedings—I don't know how to characterize it."

To which one of the defense lawyers, William Kunstler, replied: "Your Honor, we do not permit or not permit our clients. They are free independent human beings who have been brought by the Government to this courtroom."

At the end of the trial, the judge was able to state without contradiction: "I haven't heard either lawyer for the defendants try to quiet their clients during this trial when they spoke out, not once in four and a half months, not once."

Kunstler called the prosecutor "a dirty old man." The defense lawyers, despite instructions not to advise the jury of certain rulings (since these rulings would be reviewed by a higher court and should not, meanwhile, be brought to the attention of the jury), deliberately violated these instructions and informed the jury about them.

The defendants, with their counsel's connivance, indulged in antics of all sorts, intended to make impossible any decorum or dignity which should accompany the intellectual process of a trial. They insisted, for example, on their right to bring a birthday cake into the courtroom to celebrate the birthday of one of the defendants—who, incidentally, is under indictment in Connecticut for conspiring to commit murder. [The indictment against Bobby Seale was subsequently dismissed.—Ed.]

The defendants packed the courtroom with partisans who yelled derisive comments at the prosecutor and the judge, joined in bursts of loud laughter by defendants at adverse testimony, and chanted, "oink, oink," when the judge was called a pig. When any unruly spectator was ejected, curses, obscenities and threats were uttered by defendants and their adherents.

New York Panther Trial

And now we have in New York the case of the Black Panthers indicted for the bombing of two police stations, attempts at murder, twenty counts for possessing bombs, pistols and guns without licenses and conspiracy to bomb local department stores during last year's Easter season. Since they claimed that some of the evidence had been seized illegally, they were entitled to a pretrial hearing of the issue of illegal seizure. The hearing was scheduled before Supreme Court Justice John Murtagh.

The defendants and their six counsel used the same tactics that had been used in the Chicago trial, with a few ingenious variations. When they entered the courtroom, they screamed: "Power to the people!" and adherents, who had packed the courtroom, yelled either: "Power to the people!" or "Right on!" They called Justice Murtagh "fascist pig," "faggot," "gangster," "greasy pig," "insane," "fascist lackey," "buzzard," "grandee vulture," "dried-up cracker in female robes," "Hitler" and other names and obscenities too lurid to repeat.

One of the defendants yelled: "If the courtroom doesn't give us justice, Mr. Murtagh, we are going to tear this raggedly, filthy, injustice pigpen out, every single day." These were not empty threats. On two occasions, they caused melees in which they threw tables and chairs around the room. . . .

They threatened the judge continuously. . . . In one of the screaming scenes, they kicked and fought with court attendants. One detective and three policemen were hospitalized, one of them bleeding after being kicked in his kidneys. During these fights, spectators stood on their seats and screamed: "Kill the pigs." . . .

A bomb was thrown at the judge's home in upper Manhattan. The windows were blown out and the brick front scorched. There were riots near the courthouse. On the front sidewalk was painted: "Free the Panther 21." Autos were overturned. . . .

The defendants were represented by one black and five white attorneys. They approved the conduct of their clients as ideologically justified and necessary. One of them described himself as a "revolutionary lawyer" whose purpose was to "to turn the courts upside down." . . .

Justice Murtagh was unable to proceed with the hearing because witnesses could not be heard and there were riotous conditions in the courtroom. He suspended proceedings and sent the defendants back to jail until they promised to behave. [The trial ultimately ended in the acquittal of the defendants.—Ed.]

When the Chicago trial is discussed, one hears much about Judge Hoffman's conduct, and the charges that he acted in a biased, prejudicial and unfair manner. The defendants and their counsel claim that their conduct must be understood in the light of Judge Hoffman's provocation. They ignore the provocation to which they subjected him.

When [Bobby] Seale [the Black Panther leader] was finally cross-examined, for example, he conceded that during the convention he had told the people in Lincoln Park: "Pick up a gun, pull the spike from the wall, because if you pull it out and you shoot well, all I am gonna do is pat you on the back, and say: 'Keep on shooting.'" Such a defendant cannot make credible his present claim that his peaceful disposition was stirred beyond control by the judge's "unfairness." Similarly, this remark by the defendant Abbie Hoffman to the judge—". . . stick it up [your] bowling ball. How is your war stock doing, Julie?"—hardly permits the contention that the defendants would have been courteous but for their resentment of legal rulings.

Undignified Exercises

The reason I dismiss the criticism of Judge Hoffman's behavior is not that I endorse everything he did or ruled. On the contrary, his apparent resort to misstating counsel's name, and toying with sarcastic exchanges were often ineffectual as well as undignified exercises. Also, there may be serious questions about the correctness of his rulings in excluding certain witnesses and evidence.

The point is that there is full legal remedy for any error or misconduct by a judge. No judicial system in the world affords so many appeals to a convicted defendant to test the propriety of the judge's conduct and rulings—even any prejudicial comment by a prosecutor.

If the defendants and their counsel had been interested in acquittal rather than political incendiarism, they would have blessed the judge for what they claim was his open bias. The judge's alleged misbehavior was a boon to the defendants, because our protective judicial system would have turned it to their advantage.

But criticism of Judge Hoffman, even if justified, is irrelevant to the consideration of available procedure to preserve the judicial process. There is full remedy against a judge's misbehavior. There is no remedy at present for the kind of open treason to the judicial system which the defendants and their counsel committed in the cases we have been discussing here.

We have proceeded for centuries on the theory that all parties and their counsel in a trial will comply with certain rules. Those rules are sensitively constructed so that the *rights of the defendants* may be preserved. It was not anticipated that defendants would seek to escape justice by making it impossible to conduct a trial at all. That, and not Judge Hoffman's conduct, is the issue. It is this new challenge to our judicial system which must be met. . . .

There is a joke about the American system of law: "This is the only country in the world in which the defendant goes home at night and the jury is locked up." We have constructed a cordon of protection around defendants. This admirable solicitude for the accused assumes that they will honor and cherish the judicial procedure which protects them. They must not be allowed to defile that procedure and then complain that it is tainted.

It is time that we free the judge—free him from the manacles of procedures and rules which were magnificent, and still remain so, for those who will comply with the exquisite machinery constructed and refined over centuries, but inadequate to meet a new assault upon it. The time has come to provide rules that will enable the judge to control the courtroom, prevent obstruction and not suffer the frustration of helplessness lest he commit reversible error. The challenge to our judicial system, to democracy and to our sense of decency can be met.

Removing Unruly Defendants

First: Any defendant who deliberately and continuously violates decorum in the courtroom, whether by noisy outbursts, obscenities, insulting the judge or otherwise interfering with the normal conduct of the trial, may, after repeated unheeded warnings, be removed from the courtroom and placed in jail. The stenographic minutes of each day's trial shall be sent to him and his removal shall not be deemed a violation of his right not to be tried *in absentia.*

If we wish to be supermeticulous, we can arrange an open telephone line so that he can talk from jail to his lawyer; even a TV hookup, so that he can watch the proceedings. Technologically, he will be present in the courtroom.

It may be argued that this would still deprive the defendant of the right guaranteed by the Constitution to confront his accusers. If confrontation is interpreted to mean eyeball presence—yes. But if it means, as it should, full opportunity to hear the accusation, cross-examine accusing witnesses and rebut their testimony—no.

It has also been contended that a witness who sees the defendant staring at him may be inhibited from straying from the truth, and the jurors may form an impression of the defendant by watching him in the courtroom. Removing him from the courtroom deprives him of these advantages, it is said. These are questionable advantages at best and they are far outweighed by the exigencies created by the defendant himself.

I reject the proposal that such a defendant be placed in an Eichmann-like Plexiglas booth in the court. He still could distract the jurors by gesticulating or pounding against the walls. Besides, the Eichmann booth was used not to prevent his disorder, but to protect him from possible injury.

As soon as the defendant realizes, and it will be soon, that he is not achieving his objective to prevent the trial's progress, and that he is better off enjoying the comfort of the courtroom and advises the court that he will behave, he should be returned to the courtroom.

The defendant is guaranteed the right to confront his accusers so that he can be assured a fair trial. But if, by his presence, he obstructs the trial, then he destroys the reason for his privilege, and can no longer claim it. The power of the Court to remove an uncontrollably obstreperous defendant from the courtroom, without violating his constitutional rights, would preserve decent conditions at a trial and make it unnecessary to resort to clumsy, cruel shackling and gagging of a defendant—as was done at the Chicago trial.

Dealing With Obstreperous Lawyers

Second: Any lawyer who deliberately and continuously obstructs justice, collaborating with a client's misbehavior which prevents the orderly procedure of the court, may, after repeated, unheeded warnings, be removed from the trial by the judge, who may designate another defense counsel for the defendant.

This should not be deemed a violation of the defendant's constitutional right to select his own lawyer. The offending lawyer was his agent, and defendant approved his agent's defiance of the rules of the court. He cannot complain about the loss of his lawyer when he must share the responsibility for that loss.

It should be noted that we are here dealing with a rare instance. There are very few lawyers who will lend themselves to disorderly technique. They are either men who share the ideologies of their client or, for some other reason, are ready to violate their duty as officers of the court. Granting the court the authority to remove such a lawyer would be merely another step toward the court's proper preservation of the serenity of the courtroom, and would avoid the temptation for endless, vituperative exchanges.

Third: The practice of packing the courtroom with voluble adherents of the defendants must be controlled. The back of the courtroom is intended to be available for observers so that trials are public. But if partisans preempt the seats and applaud, cheer, scream and insult, sometimes in unison, the judicial process is prejudiced. Such behavior is a revolutionary tactic, violating the sanctity of reason and impartiality which should prevail in a court of justice.

Perhaps the Civil Liberties Union and similar groups should be invited to attend such trials, so as to preclude the charge that kangaroo proceedings are taking place.

Fourth: Whenever a man points an accusing finger at someone else, he has four fingers pointing at himself. We of the bar have a great responsibility which we have not met. The appellate divisions of the state and Federal courts and bar associations, which have disciplinary powers over lawyers, must act firmly, promptly and quickly to suspend or disbar any lawyer who engages in unseemly conduct involving the honor and dignity of our profession. There are very few such offending lawyers, but they should be weeded out. Contempt charges are hardly enough; they raise more questions than they answer. Furthermore, they become effectual after the trial, and therefore do not solve the trial problem except as a deterrent for the future.

Although punishment for contempt is a classic power derived from Anglo-Saxon common law, it is subject to the charge that the judge who is offended acts as both prosecutor and judge. When a jail sentence is imposed, questions of due process arise—the right of a defendant to a trial with all the safeguards for one whose liberty is at stake. While Judge Hoffman kept within well-established precedents of two-month to six-month sentences for contemptuous conduct, he multiplied the sentences by treating each offense separately —and thus cumulatively reached four-year sentences for some of the defendants and lawyers. Thus, a whole series of new questions is posed by an attempt to apply the contempt remedy—whereas, as I have suggested, the procedure should really be preventive.

In normal circumstances, it is admirable that when there is a collision between lawyer and judge, the appellate courts guard the prerogative and rights of the trial lawyer. However, the authorities who license lawyers must recognize the new and larger danger to the profession which disobedience of the law by its very practitioners presents.

Fifth: We should enact state and Federal legislation making the kind of conduct above described in a courtroom a felony—the felony of obstruction of justice. This will be the most effective deterrent of all.

If a defendant spirits away a witness, he is guilty of obstruction of justice. How much more so is there obstruction of justice by the defendants in their new tactics. If we had had such a law, the thirty Nazis and Fascists who walked out when Judge Eicher died could have been indicted and convicted of the separate crime of obstructing justice. Every lawyer who deliberately aided in the fiasco could have been indicted on the same ground—and, if found guilty, automatically disbarred.

Preserving Rights of the Accused

If we meet the new challenge by such rules as I have suggested, or by equivalent ones, then neither defendants nor their lawyers will be able to exploit the magnificent protective devices which the law provides for accused persons, so as to prevent the judicial process from functioning. Otherwise, Mafia, narcotics and other organized groups, as well as individual defendants, may adopt these techniques to frustrate trial procedure and escape by default.

We owe it to accused persons to preserve a trial procedure which is classic and protective. Whenever reforms are suggested in judicial procedure, we may expect the charge that the new measures are "repressive." Aside from the meaninglessness of such labels, can it be said that taking stronger measures to preserve the judicial system is repressive rather than protective?

If those who are interested in preserving the rights of the accused, and the traditional role of the lawyer in fighting for human rights and justice, prevent the measures necessary to defeat the tactics of revolutionaries who are determined to destroy our democratic institutions, then there will be those who will submit far harsher countermeasures. Then we may have unnecessary repressive measures in the name of saving our system of justice. To make our democratic institutions effective, within clearly defined democratic and constitutional limits is the least we can do. It is a noble task—one not to be decried as repression.

III. THUMBS ON THE SCALES OF JUSTICE: WHY THE DEFENSE CAN'T REST

EDITOR'S INTRODUCTION

Even in the most rigidly totalitarian societies, systems of justice are designed with the primary aim of apprehending, convicting, and punishing transgressors of the law. That is why authoritarian regimes tend to be models of law and order. But the American system of justice has always prided itself as much on the protection of the innocent as on the punishment of the guilty. For almost two hundred years, ever since the founding of the republic, the notion that the accused is presumed innocent until proved guilty has been a basic pillar of American law. Over that time span, the Supreme Court has worked cautiously but steadily to broaden and extend constitutional guarantees to a fair trial, equal justice, and due process of law. Today an individual accused of crime has a vast array of constitutional and legal safeguards designed to reinforce the presumption of his innocence—the right to free counsel if he is poor, to innumerable appeals to higher courts, to release without bail in some jurisdictions, especially if he is too poor to raise bond.

Despite these elaborately devised and enumerated guarantees, however, the casebooks of American law continue to be filled with instances of justice denied the innocent and rights abused. The poor, the minority groups, and in recent years many young people of a certain hair style or radical political persuasion have found justice severe, not only at the hands of police but in the nation's courtrooms as well. For all the clamor about equality, a wealthy offender can still "buy" the safeguards that exist, while the poor cannot.

The four articles in this section eloquently plead one of the contentions that our forefathers argued when they wrote the Bill of Rights: that an innocent man falsely convicted is a greater injustice than a guilty man falsely freed. In the first selection an editor of the *Saturday Review* examines official pleas for law and order and concludes that harsher laws, longer sentences, and more arrests are not the means to greater justice. In the second article Ramsey Clark, the noted civil libertarian and former United States Attorney General, argues the case against bail and preventive or pretrial detention as effective deterrents to crime. The last two articles show what can happen when such issues as skin color or national origin casually impair that presumption of innocence which supposedly is a landmark of our system.

TOUGHER LAWS ARE NOT THE ANSWER [1]

During the past two years legitimate public concern over the issue of crime, compounded by fear of campus unrest and other social disturbances, has created the volatile mixture that generally goes under the name "law and order." The rhetoric of ambitious politicians and the apparent inability—at least on occasion—of existing institutions to resolve or mitigate the issue have produced a dangerous situation. Although the nation rejected the most strident candidates of law and order in the 1970 elections and appeared far less hysterical than some analysts and commentators had supposed, considerable damage has been done, not only by the campaign and the climate it fostered, but by the specific legislative acts that preceded or accompanied it. The Democrats, goaded by the President and the attacks of the Vice President, proclaimed proudly that prior to the October recess of Congress "every major anticrime and antipornography proposal has been passed by the United States Senate." Among them:

> The Organized Crime Control Act of 1970, which
> includes a provision permitting judges to impose thirty-

[1] From "The Law-and-Order Issue," by Peter Schrag, editor-at-large. *Saturday Review*. 53:26+. N. 21, '70. Copyright 1970 Saturday Review, Inc. Reprinted by permission.

year sentences on anyone convicted of a felony if the judge decides that the defendant is "a dangerous special offender"—meaning, in simple language, when the judge concludes that the person in question is a bad guy. The bill, moreover, abridges constitutional safeguards against self-incrimination and the use of illegally obtained evidence. In its analysis of the act, the Bar Association of the City of New York declared that the bill sweeps "far beyond the field of organized crime. . . . The bill as presently drafted [and subsequently passed] frequently hits targets which were not intended and misses those which were. . . . Even more disturbing is the impatience which [the bill] shows for constitutional safeguards."

The District of Columbia Omnibus Crime Bill, now signed into law, which gives police the authority to search premises with a warrant but without announcing their presence and demanding entry (the no-knock provision) and which many lawyers regard as a violation of constitutional prohibitions against illegal search and seizure. The act also provides for preventive detention—the incarceration without bail of criminal suspects who appear, in the judgment of a magistrate, to be likely to commit further crimes if they were free. In effect, the act allows a judge to imprison a suspect before trial; although existing inequities of the money-bail system have resulted in the incarceration of thousands of legally innocent suspects, the District of Columbia act, rather than eliminating the injustices, institutionalizes them. The Administration considers it a model for the nation.

Neither of these acts nor any others recently passed by Congress deal with the substantive inadequacies of earlier crime bills, among them the Omnibus Crime Control Act of 1968, which provides for block grants to states to assist in their law-enforcement activities. A disproportionate share of the funds disbursed under that act have gone to small towns, which often use them to buy equipment and weapons they do not need and wouldn't know how to use if they did, and to state police departments, not to large urban ("high crime") areas nor for the reform and improvement of other sectors of the criminal justice process—among them the courts and correctional institutions. In all of their eagerness to improve "law enforcement," neither Congress nor the Administration has ever shown serious interest in appropriating funds to reform prisons, which happen to be the most intensive breeding grounds of crime in America.

If the problem were limited to the danger of specific congressional acts—dangers of omission and commission—it would be serious enough. But the climate produced by the rhetoric of the past year is likely to produce even more damaging effects. The cry for law and order has encouraged local prosecutors, police, and grand juries to crack down on dissenters, to intimidate unpopular figures, and to initiate criminal proceedings of dubious merit. Civil liberties organizations around the nation have noted sharp increases in the harassment of students, teachers, university administrators, writers, black people, and other minorities. Dissenters are finding it harder to get jobs or to keep them. Students—especially those with long hair—are searched at random by state police, and demonstrators are now being routinely photographed by police agents on the street.

The crime control acts passed by Congress, many of them initiated by individuals representing racial backlash, tend to hit poor people more severely than they do the affluent. It is the poor who cannot afford high-priced legal talent, cannot raise bail, and cannot defend themselves against the intricacies of the legal process; it is the poor who are more likely to be regarded as bad risks, as potential criminals, and as "dangerous special offenders." But it is also the poor—and the black—who are, and always have been, the special victims of local police raids, of unexplained shootings, and of violent acts inside or outside the station house. There have, without doubt, been unprovoked attacks on policemen during the past few months. But the equally unprovoked attacks by agents of law enforcement on unarmed black people, on the offices of political or racial organizations, and on students have received little attention from the President, the Congress, or the local agencies of law enforcement. . . .

All of these developments suggest that, so far, neither the Congress nor the Administration has seriously grappled with the really vexing problems of the processes of criminal justice. They have largely disregarded the legitimate needs of large cities for improved police methods and training, swifter administration of justice, and wholesale reform of correctional institutions (most of which are barbaric). They have tended to ignore acts of local violence against minorities and students. They have knuckled under to the gun lobby on the issue of gun control legislation. And they have consistently disregarded the recommendations of what now seems an endless series of national commissions on the reform of ghetto conditions and the enforcement of the civil rights laws.

INNOCENCE PRESUMED OR INNOCENCE DENIED? [2]

Ronnie Brown was five years old when his mother brought him north to Brooklyn from rural South Carolina. Before he was arrested on July 25, 1969, for robbery at the age of seventeen, police had taken him into custody twice— once for assault, later for car theft. He had never been convicted of a crime. On August 14, 1969, at 5:20 A.M., he was discovered dead, hanging from a light fixture in his Rikers Island prison cell—a belt looped around his neck. He had been in jail nineteen days, though no grand jury had indicted him and no lawyer had advised him of his rights, when his aunt heard of his death on the radio. She told his mother, a nurse in a VA Hospital, twelve hours before the police found time to advise her.

[2] From "Presumed Innocent? Bail and Preventive Detention," Chapter 18 of *Crime in America: Observations on Its Nature, Causes, Prevention and Control*, by Ramsey Clark, former Attorney General of the United States. Simon & Schuster. '70. p 277-94 of the Pocket Books edition. Copyright © 1970, by Ramsey Clark. Reprinted by permission of Simon & Schuster, Inc.

Ronnie had written his mother, "Dear Mom, This is not the life I want. I am not really bad. . . . I want to get out and work and do something good." He didn't explain why he was "afraid to go to the bathroom." To persons familiar with American jails, it was not necessary. He did not want to be raped by homosexuals.

Ronnie Brown, dead at age seventeen, is still presumed innocent. Can the same presumption apply to a society that permits such inhumanity? The Commissioner of Corrections reported this death as the eleventh suicide in the New York City system during the first eight months of 1969. The problem, he said, was overcrowded jails and insufficient staffs. Hundreds perish this way each year in these United States. They never include the wealthy, the worldly-wise, or the famous among us.

The purpose of the Eighth Amendment provision that "Excessive bail shall not be required" was to prevent arbitrary imprisonment before trial. Its moving spirit was the presumption of innocence—a presumption arising from the importance of the individual in the hierarchy of American values. It meant that the dignity of the individual must not be demeaned by infringement on his liberty through imprisonment unless he is convicted of crime. The Eighth Amendment was included in the Bill of Rights to insure human dignity.

Intended to confer a right of constitutional magnitude, the prohibition against excessive bail came to impose a burden. Because the Bill of Rights spoke of bail—weighing freedom against money—liberty has been denied the presumptively innocent poor. For the want of a few hundred dollars millions of impoverished Americans have suffered in jail awaiting American justice. We can sense the misery, the utter loneliness, of the minstrel immortalized in our folk music who had only one old shirt and nobody to go his bail.

The single constitutional purpose of bail is to assure the presence in court of the person charged with crime on the date his case is set for trial. Unless the defendant is present the purposes of the law are frustrated. Trial cannot be held nor innocence or guilt determined. Therefore, even though we presume the individual innocent, we require a deposit of money so he will come back for his trial—or forfeit that money. In theory, the danger that he might commit a crime before his trial is never to be considered. This would conflict with the presumption of innocence.

Why the Rich Go Free

Whatever its original concept, bail soon came to cause great and senseless injustice. Bartering liberty for money bail, the rich have been released while the poor accused of serious crime in most American jurisdictions have awaited trial in jail. It is only because they are poor that they remain in jail from arrest to trial. In the Federal system the abuses grew from the Judiciary Act in 1789 until 1966 before the first corrective action was taken by the United States Congress. For 175 years we ignored a major imperfection in our system of justice. . . .

Thousands jailed without bail were innocent. Hundreds of thousands were released after weeks or more in jail without trial. As to some, formal charges were never filed or were filed and later dismissed. Many prisoners served longer awaiting trial than the maximum sentence provided for the crime with which they were charged.

Thousands were corrupted awaiting trial in jail. Young boys, eleven or twelve years old, and teenagers were exposed to brutality, homosexual rape, drug addiction, insanity, senility and hardened human beings capable of any crime. The effect on those jailed for the first time and held for months before their trial was often to destroy their chance for rehabilitation. Many jails housed more prisoners than bunks, and some were so crowded it was difficult to find room to lie down on a cold, damp floor.

Bail was set in countless ways, but generally by formula and automatically—perhaps $100 for drunken and disorderly conduct; $1,000 for theft; $2,500 for burglary; and $10,000 for armed robbery. Often bondsmen, whose livelihood comes from the premiums determined by the amount of the bond, set bail themselves. Sometimes lawyers acting as both attorney and bondsman made bail. Defendants who could never quite pay the fee the lawyer sought would often raise the premium to make bail. There was no other way of getting out of jail. Bail premiums were a major source of income for such lawyers. . . .

How Bail Robs Society

The bail system is worse than senseless—it discriminates for no reason against the poor. Bail diverts the criminal justice system from what matters—the individual—to what doesn't—his money. Rather than asking does he need treatment, has he violated parole, should he be supervised, might he leave the country, or is he dangerous, bail asks only—does he have $500? . . .

The amount of liberty lost because of bail has been immense. The Federal Government detains fewer than 2 percent of the prisoners held pending trial on any given day in the United States. In early 1963, several years before Federal bail reform legislation was enacted, Attorney General Robert F. Kennedy instructed the United States Attorneys to exercise personal initiative in recommending the release of accused persons on their personal recognizance whenever they were satisfied that there was no substantial risk the defendant would fail to appear for trial. Prior to March 1963 only 6 percent of all persons arrested and charged with a Federal crime were released on their own recognizance without money bail. By March 1964 the percentage had nearly tripled, and by April 1, 1965, it stood at 39 percent. Between March 1964 and April 1965 the percentage of all prisoners denied release on bail or on their personal assurances declined from 37 to 8.5 percent.

During those years the average pretrial detention per prisoner was forty-one days. By a single administrative directive approximately 9,000 persons were saved forty-one days each during the course of a year—369,000 days of liberty, 1,000 man-years. The meaning of this when applied to state and local systems is staggering. Hundreds of thousands of people are detained in jails before trial every year.

The release of these thousands of people actually lowered the rate at which defendants failed to appear for trial. The rate of bail jumping in the Federal system by those with enough money to make bail had been 3 percent nationwide. Nearly 98 percent of the individuals released on their personal promise to appear voluntarily came to court for their trials. The poor, theretofore held in jail before trial because they could not post a few hundred or a few thousand dollars, showed up for trial voluntarily with greater frequency than those who had been released on money bail.

In one Federal court, the Eastern District of Michigan, 84 percent of all prisoners accused of crime were released without bail in 1965. Only 1 out of the 711 thus released defaulted. With care this record could be equaled throughout the country. . . .

The Case Against Pretrial Detention

The public is reminded again and again of the cases where a person released pending trial is charged with another crime. Demagogues and those who seek easy solutions to crime while opposing the expense of essential action dramatize the stupidity of a system that cannot cope with such an obvious problem. We are urged to ignore the principles we profess—that every American is presumed innocent until proven guilty—and it is proposed that we jail the accused until his trial, because somehow we know he is a danger to society.

We call the proposal preventive detention. It would keep many persons accused of crime in jail pending trial. Preventive detention is neither necessary nor desirable to control crime. [For another view on this subject, see "The Case for Pretrial Detention," in Section IV, below.—Ed.] Inconsistent with our basic principles, it would deter correction of major defects in our system of criminal justice, violate important constitutional rights of citizens, and tend to cause crime. A glance at history and present practice tells us why.

Under a system of preventive detention, fear instead of money would determine whether an accused is to be released. In practice it would operate much like bail. In times of great concern over crime, bail has usually been set not at a norm or to assure appearance at trial but deliberately high to prevent release. During "crime waves," many judges release few people on bail. This is a part of the hypocrisy of the bail system. Under such circumstances bail has nothing to do with its stated purpose—to assure the presence of the defendant at trial—but is a judge's way of protecting the public from people he believes dangerous and himself from criticism.

If preventive detention is authorized, courts acting from community fear will release very few people when crime concerns the public. Poor and unpopular groups and individuals—the Black Panthers, the Weathermen, ghetto dwellers —would be most affected. The test for a judge or magistrate in deciding whether to jail or release under a preventive detention statute—Will the defendant pose a danger to the community?—is necessarily subjective. His burden is greater than a jury's after trial, for juries at least have a rational assignment. They do not have to predict future human conduct. Juries determine past facts. There is yet little evidence that we can predict what people will do in the future. But the consequences of a decision to detain a person in jail until his trial may often be as dire as a verdict of guilt. A year in jail awaiting trial can be worse than a year on a prison farm after conviction.

Preventive detention could easily result in massive, destructive, needless jailing. The history of bail tells us what is possible. Have we overcome our capacity for neglect? It is tradition, not words, that protects rights. What good do the words of the Eighth Amendment do the poor southern Negro or the urban slum dweller? Only the firmest commitment against unnecessary and wrongful detention will avoid filling jails with hundreds of thousands of people not proven guilty while we tell our young we presume all to be innocent. Strong traditions that inhibit officials from jailing persons before trial will force us to make the reforms essential to both justice and security. These include assurance of a speedy trial, jail and prison reform, and indeterminate sentencing procedures. Preventive detention will impede those reforms. . . .

The Problem of Repeaters

Pretrial detention is not necessary to protect the public —even if it could—for a number of important reasons. The first and most critical has to do with the sentencing process itself. The greater part of all serious crime is committed by repeaters. It is these very repeaters who are least likely to be released pending trial. They constitute probably 95 percent of the persons judges or magistrates in a properly functioning system would hesitate to release pending trial. The reason is that their future is predicted from their past. If the defendant is a four-time loser and suspected of many other crimes, he is expected, barring evidence of some change, to be capable of further crime.

But if he has been convicted before of any crime showing a capability to do serious harm, society had its best chance, indeed duty, to prevent him from committing further crime. If he has committed another crime, the system had failed. A correctional program tailored to his particular needs, based on a flexible sentence imposed to provide the opportunity for continuous effort, provides the best chance for rehabilitation. The only sentence that can do this is the indeterminate sentence.

The indeterminate sentence fixes an outer limit of potential imprisonment—five years or ten years, for example— but empowers correctional authorities to release the defendant whenever they believe he is capable of living in society without committing antisocial acts. Under such a sentence, professional supervisors can impose conditions of release designed to rehabilitate the releasee and prevent him from engaging in criminal acts. In a properly functioning system, most defendants might spend as much as 90 percent of their sentences in community environments and half of their time without significant restraints on their liberty. Rehabilitating offenders through prison reform would greatly reduce instances where preventive detention might be used—and greatly reduce crime itself.

Any program will have failures. When a person serving an indeterminate sentence is accused of a subsequent crime, he can be taken into custody for violation of the conditions of his parole if there is evidence he has done so. If he has violated those conditions—perhaps by failing to return to a dormitory, by dropping out of school, by associating with the old gang or by being on the street at 2 A.M.—parole supervisors should know it before the police do. When they don't, the police can advise them. Society has a claim on his freedom for past wrongful conduct. The accused is entitled to due process in any parole revocation procedure, but the issue is whether he violated conditions of parole, not whether another crime was committed. There is no trial as such and no requirement of evidence beyond a reasonable doubt. If another crime has been committed, the earlier program has obviously failed and should be immediately redesigned in the light of new evidence. The offender, rather than being kept in jail until he is tried on new charges, should be placed in a correctional program based on professional estimates of need considering all the circumstances. Certainly, if he seems dangerous, he will not be released without supervision.

The use of indeterminate sentencing and community correctional control is slight and ineffective today. Nearly all felons spend the final years of their sentences at large. The time ranges from two thirds in most Federal cases to one third in nearly all jurisdictions. While they are technically on parole, they are as a practical matter without supervision. The period of time on parole is longer and involves far greater opportunity for crime than the time between arrest and trial. Parole is the time of greatest risk of recidivism, because if further crimes are likely to be committed, they are most likely to occur soon after a prisoner is released from prison and placed on parole. Crime repetition becomes steadily less likely with the passage of time....

Who Gets Detained?

Under existing law there are three important classes of crime where the issue of preventive detention is not presented. Combined, they eliminate any remaining vestige of rationality in preventive detention and offer an opportunity for an effective resolution of the pretrial detention dilemma.

In capital cases throughout our history we have reserved the power to detain an accused pending trial. The Eighth Amendment was written and ratified against a background permitting detention of persons charged with capital crimes. Money bail, it was thought, might not assure the appearance of a defendant charged with crime where life itself was at stake. Life was the only thing this theory valued above money.

In practical terms this rule means that persons accused of the most serious offenses—murder, rape, armed robbery, assault with intent to kill and other major crimes of violence —for which the death penalty can be invoked need not be, and are rarely, if ever, released pending trial in most states. Wrong in principle, the practice has at least the gloss of history and because it is limited to very serious crimes is preferable to an untested technique of preventive detention. It provides a better basis for public protection than preventive detention, pending accomplishment of essential reforms. But it should be abandoned.

Second, preventive detention authority is not needed to detain juveniles. The law will develop in time to grant ju-

veniles more of the protections afforded adults under the
Constitution. Today, however, juveniles can be and are arbitrarily detained pending trial on criminal charges. Indeed,
they are often detained without the formality of charges, as
when the state stands in the place of the parent where there
are allegations of neglect or delinquency. Curfews, compul-
sory schooling and juvenile detention homes often restrict
the freedom of the young without trial or due process. While
these practices are themselves wrong, they afford a protection
today that gives time for needed reform of the judicial
system without resorting to a new expanded pretrial custody.

Finally, preventive detention does not address itself to
the problem of the mentally deranged. There are madmen
who can pose a danger to the community. But they are not
made sane by holding them in jail pending trial. Indeed, if
incompetent, they may not face trial. Their need is for
medical judgment and treatment and the issue is not whether
to release or detain them pending trial, but one of health
or sickness. The lines between mental commitment and
trial for a crime are not precise, and clearly the present judicial techniques of determining mental capacity are fraught
with risk and full of abuse, but preventive detention has no
relevance to the problems of crime by the mentally ill. They
are detained today through procedures of commitment designed to determine their sanity, without regard to whether
they might commit a crime.

Need for Community Supervision

The remaining potential for crime by persons released
between arrest and trial is slight but the public has additional protection without jailing persons presumed innocent.
A well-financed and adequately staffed community supervision agency can provide services that reduce the chance
of crime by employing techniques for pretrial release used
effectively in parole and probation cases. Services will include health care, school, vocational training, job placement,

counseling and family assistance. Conditions under which an accused is released and which he must obey to remain at liberty can reduce the risks of crime. Some conditions are designed to assure presence at trial and do not infringe on the assumption of innocence. Other conditions may be acceptable to an accused and therefore raise no legal issues. If necessary, special surveillance can be ordered by a court.

Conditions of release have included room inspection, requirements that the accused be at home at night, daily observation of conduct, checking presence at employment, school and home, restrictions on associations, and regular reporting in by phone or at an office designated by the court.

Civil commitments for alcoholics and addicts that give some supervisory power over an individual but avoid the stigma of criminal charges may be substituted entirely for criminal prosecution, or applied in modified forms for pretrial purposes. These same techniques of supervision, essential to successful probation and parole, are also meaningful in some pretrial situations. They are clearly the greatest restrictions society can justly place on an individual where, even on a finding of guilt, probation or a short jail sentence is the most severe sentence probable.

Until the last few years no supervision of persons released on bail was possible. There was no one to provide it. The choice was jail or unrestricted freedom. With bail reform, staffs capable of supervising accused persons released pending trial have been established. Strong bail agencies, professionally staffed with adequate manpower, will reduce crime, while pretrial jailing will often cause crime. Agencies to supervise persons between arrest and trial should become an important part of our system, closely coordinated with police, prosecution, courts and corrections.

Need for Speedy Trials

Then, there is the absolute necessity for an early trial. The Bill of Rights was concerned primarily with the rights

of the accused when it sought to assure what is usually denied—a speedy trial.

Clearly now, the public safety as well depends on speedy
trial. A chief deterrent of the entire activity of the system
of criminal justice is lost when months or years elapse between crime and conviction. The only time the average
person will see any connection between his criminal act and
the consequences of conviction is when conviction follows
the criminal act quickly.

A speedy trial is a far greater deterrent than a lengthy
sentence. Longer criminal sentences are often imposed when
public concern over crime is high. This is a reaction of courts
to the public's, and perhaps the courts' own, concern. But
it is an emotional reaction. Long sentences have not deterred
crime. The question is not how long the sentence, but what
happens to the individual while he serves it. Is he rehabili-
tated or hardened?

If many months pass between the criminal act and a
conviction, the connection between the two is remote and
seems happenchance. Punishment, as the punished view it,
does not follow swiftly and inexorably from crime. The
greatest deterrent for the person capable of committing
crime is the belief, when he decides whether to act, that if
he does he will be quickly apprehended and convicted as a
direct result of his conduct.

Preventive detention would tend to prolong the time
between arrest and trial. In addition to relieving the pressure
for speedy trial, preventive detention would require additional hearings that courts are ill equipped to handle. Should
the accused be released? Is he dangerous? What facts has the
prosecution assembled that show he is dangerous? What
evidence has the defense to show he is not? What of appeals
from decisions denying release? Is this the way courts should
spend their time?

An early trial reduces the risk that an accused will commit another crime pending trial. If trials are held within

sixty days instead of sixteen months, the opportunity for additional crimes is reduced.

With conviction, the presumption of innocence is lost. Then the burden is on the individual to prove that his trial was unfair, or that he is not guilty. Accordingly, there is no right to release from custody while a case is on appeal just as there is no right of appeal. Once the accused is convicted, the question of release pending an appeal is at the discretion of the court. Danger to the community may be a factor in the court's decision, though the overriding question is the probability of reversal. In practice, courts generally provide for the release of persons convicted pending appeal. Only rarely are the rich and powerful such as leaders of La Cosa Nostra denied bail pending appeal. This illustrates the discrimination inherent in pretrial detention.

Lethargy pervades human conduct and institutional reform. Pressures are necessary to produce essential action. Preventive detention would relieve just those pressures that will force reforms far more important to public safety than the insignificant and doubtful security it can offer. We can accomplish needed reform safely without reliance on preventive detention. . . .

Upholding the Presumption of Innocence

If we reform prisons, protect the public from crime by repeaters through indeterminate sentencing, provide speedy trials and adequately staff bail-supervision agencies, how great is the risk of crime by persons awaiting trial? If we fail to make these reforms, can preventive detention—which denies human dignity, keeps youngsters out of school, breaks up families and exposes persons to jail brutality—reduce crime? If during the time required to make essential reforms in judicial administration and prison and jail reform the public is protected from crimes committed between arrest and trial by repeaters, by persons charged with capital crimes, by juveniles and by the criminally insane, is there any need for preventive detention?

The presumption of innocence should not be lightly discarded. It has elemental force. Its spirit is embodied in the Eighth Amendment. It establishes the relationship between the individual and the state, implying that every person is worth something, may have dignity and be deserving of trust. In questions between citizen and state, the presumption is—and must remain—that the individual will prevail until society proves him a criminal beyond a reasonable doubt. He cannot be jailed on suspicion, nor held pending investigation and trial, merely because he is poor, or even if he is despised. The Nixon Administration has referred to the presumption of innocence as a "mere rule of procedural evidence." Liberty and human dignity will never be secure among a people who place so little value on so fundamental a principle.

In these turbulent times, when the individual is easily lost, when he can do so little to affect things vital to his very being, actions that depreciate his dignity are extremely harmful. The young, the educated, the disadvantaged in mass society sense the heavy pall on their chance to be somebody, to do something, to fulfill themselves. They sense our hypocrisy, professing one thing, practicing another. They sense how slowly our institutions change to meet clear needs —our reluctance to make vital reforms. Preventive detention would be a tragic step backward at a time when we must move swiftly on.

ANNALS OF LAW: BE JUST AND FEAR NOT [3]

E. J. KAHN, JR.

Shortly before midnight on Thursday, August 20th, Thomas Goins, a light-skinned black man who works as a chauffeur and valet for an investment banker and lives with his employer at 1001 Park Avenue, was feeling glum. He

[3] Article on the perils of false arrest by E. J. Kahn, Jr., staff writer. *New Yorker.* 46:76-84. F. 6, '71. Reprinted by permission; © 1971 The New Yorker Magazine, Inc.

had been stood up. Goins, a thirty-eight-year-old bachelor, had been given the night off by his boss, Derek D. Grewcock, a general partner in Loeb, Rhoades & Co., at 42 Wall Street. At nine-thirty, after changing from his chauffeur's uniform into a sports shirt and slacks, Goins had parked Grewcock's car, a 1970 Lincoln Continental, in a garage on East Eighty-fourth Street and had driven his own car, a 1968 Buick, to the upper Bronx, where he had a date with a Telephone Company employee who worked nights. They had agreed to meet at a street corner when she got off, at ten-thirty. Goins arrived promptly, waited an hour, cursed womankind, and started home. He planned to get on the Major Deegan Expressway, southbound, at its Yankee Stadium approach. Now, close to twelve o'clock, he was hungry. On his way back home to eat, he thought he might like to have some ginger ale with his supper. Then he remembered that he had drunk the last of the ginger ale at 1001 Park the day before. So Goins drove slowly down Ogden Avenue, parallel to the Major Deegan, hoping to find a store open. Ogden Avenue runs through a middle-class, predominantly Irish neighborhood, with the homes of blue-collar workers scattered among small stores. At the northwest corner of Ogden and 165th Street, Goins spotted a bar that was open—McCann & Whelan's Tavern. Goins pulled to the curb, in a metered parking space. Leaving his headlights on, he entered the tavern, where the bartender on duty, Robert Brewer, was chatting with half a dozen customers, most of them regulars. Goins asked for a quart bottle of ginger ale. Brewer didn't have any quarts, but he obligingly sold Goins three splits. Carrying them outside in a paper bag, Goins was about to get back into his car when, in the beam of its headlights, he noticed a manila envelope propped against the curb.

Goins picked up the envelope. It had no identifying marks on it. It was secured by a string wound around a tab. Standing in front of his car, Goins opened it. Inside were three packages wrapped in silver foil. "At first, I thought to myself, Someone must have thrown this away," he said later.

"But then I thought, No, that's not possible; it's too neat. So I opened the tinfoil around one of the packages." Inside that, separated into a dozen or more stacks with rubber bands around them, were a number of tiny glassine envelopes—six hundred in all, by subsequent count—each measuring about an inch and a half by a half inch, and each containing a white powder. It didn't take much perspicacity to surmise that the contents were drugs—six hundred and sixty-three grains of heroin, it developed, or slightly more than one ounce. Goins could have put the manila envelope back where he found it and driven home; most people probably would have. But while growing up, in Southern Pines, North Carolina, he was imbued with public-spiritedness. His father, who was in the construction business until he was laid low by a stroke, in 1965, had five children, and he brought them all up to be good citizens. His oldest child, a daughter, is a supervisory nurse in an Army hospital at Fort Bragg. Of his four sons, all but Thomas, the fourth child, finished college. One is now a deputy United States marshal in Raleigh, North Carolina, one runs a night club in Southern Pines, and one is an Army major piloting helicopters in Vietnam. Thomas himself spent ten years in the Army, as an enlisted man, rising to the rank of sergeant first class. It is a family with a deep-rooted interest in and respect for authority, and Thomas Goins' reaction, as he stood in front of his car in the Bronx, was that he should hand over to the police whatever it was he had found.

Goins turned toward the tavern, which has a picture window fronting on the avenue. Waving the envelope, he attracted the attention of one of the patrons, whose name, he later learned, was John McGuire. McGuire, in fact, had already followed Goins outside with his eyes; a black man buying ginger ale in an Irish bar at midnight was, after all, an unusual neighborhood occurrence. McGuire came outside. Goins showed him his find and said he thought the police should be notified. McGuire agreed. They went back inside, where McGuire borrowed a dime from Brewer, the bartender, and called the police on a pay phone. He said a fellow there had just found a suspicious-looking envelope, and asked if the police would send somebody around. After ten or fifteen minutes had gone by with no response, Goins recalled that as he drove toward the bar he had seen a fire-house on the opposite side of Ogden, half a block north of McCann & Whelan's. (Engine Company 68 and Ladder Company 49 are berthed there.) On the premise that it is easier to get action from one arm of the law by invoking another, Goins decided to walk, ginger ale in one hand and heroin in the other, to the firehouse. Arriving there, he explained what had happened to a dispatcher at a switch-board just inside the entrance. The dispatcher wouldn't phone the police, though, without the blessing of a superior, and he summoned Lieutenant Patrick G. Dwyer. The Lieu-tenant heard Goins out and called the police.

In a few minutes, a patrol car drew up. It was a car that had responded, belatedly, to the call from the tavern. As the Police Department has pieced it together, the 44th Pre-cinct, at 1278 Sedgwick Avenue, had had a call from a "male Negro" that someone was trying to sell narcotics at the bar —which was not at all what McGuire had said—and the cruiser had gone to McCann & Whelan's. Brewer had told the two patrolmen in the car to go on up to the firehouse. Arriving there, the patrolmen entered, and the officer who took charge of the proceedings, Patrolman Julius Dengler, asked Goins, "Are you the man with the drugs?" When Goins said "Yes," Dengler told him to bring along his envelope and come with them to their station house. Goins tried to tell the officers his story, but they didn't seem to want to hear it. So, clutching both his packages, he got into the back seat of the patrol car and the other policeman got in beside him; Dengler drove to the station house. Goins wasn't espe-cially perturbed. The police weren't rough; surely they couldn't be meaning to arrest him, because they hadn't even searched him. He assumed that the trip to the station house was part of some bureaucratic red tape required when people turned in drugs. As the patrol car started north on Ogden Avenue, though, Gains remembered that his car was unlocked and the headlights were still on. When he told the police that, Dengler made a U-turn and stopped at the tavern. Dengler got out, switched off the lights, and locked the car. It all happened so quickly that no one in the tavern noticed anything. Then Goins was driven to the station house, in silence.

At the 44th Precinct, Goins was booked and finger-printed and taken into an upstairs room for questioning. He was delighted to have a chance finally to tell his story to the proper authorities, and he says he did so, while various policemen filled out various forms. (The police have since contended that he remained silent, and that if he had complained loudly he might have been spared a lot of inconvenience. But few people consider it smart tactics to shout in police stations.) The only thing that bothered Goins was that he was fast running out of cigarettes. While he was being interrogated, one of the officers dumped the contents of the manila envelope onto a desk, and as policemen came in and out of the room (there was a change of shifts at midnight and the fourth platoon came in at 2 A.M., and traffic was heavy) they kept picking up the glassine envelopes and examining them—a sloppy way, in any circumstances, of handling possible evidence. Nobody seemed interested in the paper bag with the ginger ale in it. The cops asked Goins if he used drugs himself, and he said no, never. They did not seem to care much about his story. All that the police interrogating him had to go on was a complaint that Patrolman Dengler had sworn to when he reached the station house; in it there was no mention of a tavern or a firehouse. What Dengler had vouchsafed, on a complaint headed "Criminal Possession—Dangerous Drug," was that he had arrested Goins at 1:05 A.M. at 165th Street and Ogden Avenue (he was wrong by half a block), and had followed this site identification with the word "street" in parentheses—conceivably to give himself an out if anybody ever accused him of entering premises without a warrant. "The deponent states," Dengler went on, meaning himself, "that at the above-mentioned time, date, and place of occurrence the defendant [here he meant "deponent," but it was late, and he may have been tired] did observe the defendant in possession of a quantity of heroin in excess of one (1) ounce." The emphasis on "street" was to become important, because if the description had any validity Goins was a liar, and if it didn't Dengler was less than completely accurate. (The police themselves challenge this technicality; they say the use of "street" as the "place of occurrence" was justified because the original phone call referred to that location; but, in any event, Dengler never *observed* Goins at that intersection until he put out the lights of his car.) The quantity of narcotics involved was equally important, or could have been, for to knowingly have in one's possession an ounce or more of heroin is to become chargeable with a first-degree Class C felony, and a person convicted of such a crime can be sentenced to as much as fifteen years in a jail.

Most policemen are not experts on drugs, nor do they need to be. Confronted with a narcotics case, they customarily call in narcotics specialists, and in this instance they could readily have summoned one. But the drugs Goins had found didn't amount to much, by present-day standards. The six hundred packets of heroin would have retailed at three to five dollars each, but how could the police have been expected to make a fuss over this small cache of the stuff when not long before, also in the Bronx, a man had been picked up with twenty-two *pounds* on him? So the cops acted on their own in handling Goins. For his part, although he had become increasingly apprehensive about their seeming lack of appreciation of his good citizenship, it didn't occur to him that he was being booked on a narcotics charge until, at about two-thirty in the morning, he was told that he would be allowed one telephone call. Every American

knows what *that* means. The police said they would make
the call for him, and Goins gave them Grewcock's name
and number. A few minutes later Goins was handcuffed and
taken in another police car to the Bronx House of Detention, at 653 River Avenue. He never saw the ginger ale again.

Grewcock was asleep when his phone rang. An urbane
Englishman who was a vice-president of the American Ex-
press Company until he joined Loeb, Rhoades, in 1954, he
had been Goins' employer since the fall of 1967. The two
men had met at Fire Island that summer: Grewcock was
spending a holiday there with the son of a recently terminated marriage; Goins was head bartender at The Club at
Point o' Woods. The Club's manager also ran a hotel in
North Carolina and regularly moved part of his staff north
for the Fire Island summer season. It was Goins' fifth summer there. Grewcock had been looking for a valet and chauffeur, and to find one who was also a full-fledged drinkmaker
was a dividend indeed. Moreover, Grewcock was engaged to
a young woman who comes from North Carolina, and he
therefore had a particularly high regard for Goins.

Grewcock, consequently, was distressed when the police
called him, and as soon as he was awake enough to think,
he was certain that whoever it was on the phone muttering
about "possession of narcotics" must be kidding. "It was
inconceivable to me that Tom could do what the police
alleged he had done," he said afterward. Grewcock asked
what would happen next, and was told that Goins would
be arraigned at ten that morning in Bronx Criminal Court.
Grewcock said he would have a lawyer there.

As head of his firm's international department, Grewcock tries to make his schedule dovetail somewhat with
Bourse hours in Europe. Accordingly, he rises early and
—ordinarily with Goins at the wheel—reaches his Wall Street
office at about eight. On the morning of Friday, August 21st,
Grewcock drove the Continental downtown himself. He has
been living in the United States for twenty-one years, and
knows his way around. "If all else fails, I could be a chauf-

feur," he told an acquaintance during the recent market slump. Short of sleep and worried, he reached his office at eight-fifteen. Within a few minutes, ignoring London, Paris, and Amsterdam, he was on the phone to Leonard Wacksman, an early-bird downtown attorney. Wacksman's firm, Loeb, Block & Wacksman, does not engage much in criminal law, but Grewcock had thrown a lot of legal business its way, and Wacksman was anxious to help in an emergency. By nine o'clock, he had retained Arnold J. Kaplan, a midtown attorney who does specialize in criminal law. Kaplan phoned Grewcock and said that although he himself had to take part in a trial that day, he would have an associate present when Goins was arraigned, at ten. The only trouble was that Goins did not appear in Bronx Criminal Court at that hour, or at any hour that day, and throughout the day the chauffeur's swiftly appointed lawyers were unable to find a trace of him.

Goins had been kept moving since his arrest. When he was first put in a cell, at around three o'clock in the morning, his main concern had been that he was down to two cigarettes; he had asked a prison attendant if he could buy some, and had been told that it was too late. The attendant's main concern had appeared to be that Goins should remove his shoes and belt. These were placed on the floor outside his cell, which contained a toilet and a wooden bench but no bed. Not that that mattered; he was in no mood to sleep. At 7:30 A.M., he was offered an egg sandwich and some coffee. He drank the coffee. It was too early to buy cigarettes, he was told. He was taken by cruiser to Police Headquarters, on Centre Street, in Manhattan, where he was photographed and put in a detention room with fifteen other men, from one of whom he bummed a couple of cigarettes. At 1 P.M., he was offered a cheese sandwich and coffee. He again skipped the sandwich. At 4:30 P.M., with no explanation, he was handcuffed, linked by a long chain to several other manacled prisoners, put in a police van, and taken back to the Bronx, where he was again locked up in a cell. After a couple of hours there, he was removed from that cell, remanacled, and returned to Manhattan. This time, he ended up in the antechamber of a courtroom in the Criminal Court Building, also on Centre Street. Having arrived through a vehicular delivery entrance, Goins missed some of the lofty slogans that are chiselled in marble outside that structure for the edification of pedestrians: "EVERY PLACE IS SAFE TO HIM WHO LIVES IN JUSTICE," and "ONLY THE JUST MAN ENJOYS PEACE OF MIND," and "BE JUST AND FEAR NOT." By now, Goins had begun to be depressed, but mainly he was incredulous. "I simply didn't believe that anything that had happened to me could have happened," he said later.

Goins remained in the antechamber until about 2 A.M. Then, twenty-four hours after his arrest, he was brought before a Criminal Court judge. The district attorney on duty that night routinely presented the charge against him; the D.A. had no first-hand knowledge of the incident—merely Patrolman Dengler's complaint. The judge asked Goins what he did for a living, and after replying Goins began to try to tell his story. But the D.A. cut in to say that there was nothing on the charge sheet about any tavern or firehouse; according to the record, the accused had been picked up in the street, and, in view of the seriousness of the alleged crime, bail should be fixed at thirty thousand dollars. The judge asked Goins if his employer would go bond for him, and Goins said he hoped so. The judge thereupon instructed a Legal Aid attorney to phone Grewcock. Awakened for the second night running, Grewcock said yes, of course he would post bond; he had been trying to find Goins all day so he *could* bail him out. Before Grewcock went to bed, he had been on the phone for several hours, calling houses of detention all over the place to see if any of them might own up to custody of his man, and had got nowhere. Now, having been roused early on the morning of Saturday, the twenty-second, Grewcock woke up Kaplan at *his* home and asked him to make arrangements for bail as quickly as possible.

The judge, on learning that Grewcock would stand behind Goins, said that he wished he could believe the chauffeur's story and set him free then and there, but that in
the absence of the arresting officer (Patrolman Dengler was
presumably getting some sleep himself, after the previous
night's law enforcement), and in view of the arresting officer's oath that he had picked Goins up on the street, he
had no choice but to hold the suspect for trial. The judge
would, however, set bail at twenty-five thousand dollars,
which is fairly low for a heroin offense in the one-ounce
category. Goins was removed from the courtroom, handcuffed again, and, at about 5 A.M., trundled off to the
Riker's Island penitentiary, where he drank some coffee but
declined a jelly sandwich. He had no cigarettes of his own,
and he had been through two nights and a day without food
or sleep. He stayed there only about four hours, and then
resumed his travels, ending up back at the Bronx House of
Detention.

At 9 A.M., Grewcock, who didn't have to go to work on
Saturday and had gratefully gone back to sleep, was awakened
by a phone call from Kaplan. The lawyer had got hold of
Mrs. Ida Schenkman, a bail bondsman, and she would
arrange bail, but only if Grewcock came in person to her
office, on White Street, near the Manhattan Criminal Court
Building. Grewcock sighed, rose, dressed, and drove downtown. Satisfied that he was a responsible citizen, Mrs.
Schenkman accepted his personal check for twelve hundred
and fifty dollars as a surety bond. By the time she arranged
to have the necessary documents drawn up to get Goins
out of prison, it was midday. Grewcock drove back uptown,
picked up his fiancée, and went on with her to the Bronx
House of Detention, where the emergence of an attractive
young woman from a Lincoln Continental, whose driver
had inadvertently tried to park in the chief warden's reserved space, drew cackles and whistles from the inmates
surveying the parking lot from behind their bars. Goins,
whose cell view was not panoramic, had no way of knowing

that any of the bail business was going on, and it came as a surprise to him when, at about one-thirty, a guard told him to get ready to leave. A few minutes later, after signing some papers, Goins walked through a door and saw his boss. Goins burst into tears. After he had stopped crying Grewcock, sensing that he was still too unstrung to drive, put him in the back seat, gave him a package of cigarettes he had thoughtfully brought along, and drove him to 1001 Park Avenue. Inside the apartment was a "WELCOME HOME, TOM" sign that Grewcock had hastily fashioned. Goins had something to eat and went to bed.

Goins did not get a chance to sleep long. Almost as soon as they reached the apartment, Grewcock phoned Kaplan, who was standing by. The lawyer knew only what Goins had been charged with, and wanted to hear his client's version of the incident. So after Goins had had an hour's nap Grewcock woke him, and Goins phoned Kaplan. After hearing a somewhat abridged version of the tale, Kaplan urged Goins to go back to the scene of the crime, or non-crime; if there was going to be a trial, the lawyer wanted the names of possible witnesses for Goins—the bartender, the bar patrons, the fire Lieutenant, anyone else who could be of help. Goins was glad to go; for one thing, he wanted to retrieve his car. He took the subway to the Bronx and, on approaching Ogden Avenue and 165th Street, saw, to his relief, that the Buick was where he had left it. He walked into McCann & Whelan's Tavern. Robert Brewer, the bartender, wasn't on duty, but he was sitting in a booth, and when Goins appeared he jumped up and asked where he had been. In jail, Goins said.

"I knew something had happened," Brewer said. "I noticed your car was still here, and I kept an eye on it whenever the meter maid came around." The car never was ticketed; the police are more aggressive in some respects than others. Brewer said he would certainly be a witness for Goins if he stood trial, and he gave the chauffeur the name and address of John McGuire, the man who had borrowed the dime and called the cops. Next, Goins went to the firehouse. The Lieutenant who had called the police at Goins' request —Patrick Dwyer—was off duty; a lieutenant on duty suggested that Goins come back in half an hour. Goins returned to McCann & Whelan's. By now, McGuire had wandered in, and he volunteered whatever testimonial services he might be able to render. (So, a little later, did another of the Thursday-night bar patrons, Joseph Kavanaugh.) Goins asked Brewer and McGuire if they would mind having a word with his lawyer. It was noisy in the tavern, so the three men repaired to a luncheonette a few doors down Ogden. Goins got Kaplan on the phone and put Brewer and then McGuire on; each verified Goins' story. Then Goins revisited the fire station. The lieutenant he had talked with half an hour earlier said that he had consulted his captain who had said something about hearing something about a guy with a package, but that there was no pertinent entry in the firehouse log, and since there wasn't the firemen would prefer not to get involved. "Lieutenant, they got me charged up to the eyes," Goins said. "How can you say you don't want to have anything to do with it? At least give me the name of the Lieutenant who was on duty that night." The lieutenant he was talking with refused. Goins backtracked to the luncheonette and passed this sobering new intelligence along to Kaplan. If he couldn't prove he had been in the firehouse, he asked, how could he prove he hadn't been on the street? The lawyer said not to worry—he himself could always get the name of the fire Lieutenant, and if the Lieutenant wouldn't talk voluntarily he could be subpoenaed. Relieved, and, in any event, too near exhaustion to give the matter more thought, Goins climbed into his car, drove home, went back to bed, and slept through most of Sunday.

On being arraigned in Night Court, Goins had been ordered to appear in Bronx Criminal Court on Monday, August 24th, to have a date set for his trial. When Goins duly turned up there, it was comforting to have Kaplan beside him. The lawyer tried to explain to the presiding judge what had happened, but the judge wouldn't listen to him. He said he didn't have time to; his calendar was too crowded. Kaplan persisted; this was a highly unusual case, he said— one unlike anything he had come across in eighteen years of criminal-law practice. The judge cut him off and set October 5th as the trial date. Kaplan and Goins then went together to the Ogden Avenue firehouse, where, after a brief wait, they were able to talk to Lieutenant Dwyer. He wasn't particularly communicative, but when Kaplan pressed him on whether the firehouse episode Goins described had actually occurred, the Lieutenant finally said it had. That was all the lawyer needed: he had a clinching witness. Later, Kaplan also caught up with Patrolman Dengler. The policeman stuck to his story—he more or less had to, since he had sworn to it—of having picked up Goins on the street. Kaplan asked how the police had learned to begin with that Goins was on the street, or anywhere else, carrying narcotics. Through a telephone call, Dengler replied. "Of *course* that was how," Kaplan said. "*He* called *you.*"

The next day, August 25th, Kaplan got to brooding. Here he had a client who was manifestly innocent—a client who, moreover, had been falsely arrested while trying to do a good deed—and he began to wonder what might happen if, say, Goins got involved in an automobile accident while he had a serious criminal charge pending. What might the police do *then?* So Kaplan phoned Burton B. Roberts, the Bronx County District Attorney. Roberts' office would be in charge of the prosecution if Goins came to trial, but Kaplan felt confident that if the D.A. would take time to listen there would be no trial. Roberts invited Kaplan to stop by on the twenty-eighth, and when Kaplan did he urged the D.A. to conduct his own investigation and either confirm or disprove Goins' story. Roberts immediately assigned an assistant district attorney named Thomas O'Malley to the case. It didn't take O'Malley long to seek out all the witnesses and to discover that Goins' account of what had happened checked out in every detail, with the single exception of the text of the police complaint. On September 2nd, Goins had to go to the D.A.'s office to make a statement. Grewcock, who was leaving for Asia that day to open a Loeb, Rhoades branch office in Hong Kong, hired a limousine to take him to the airport. While the banker was still in Asia, O'Malley and Roberts agreed that Goins had been the victim of a terrible miscarriage of justice, and in one of the cablegrams Grewcock received from his New York office on September 15th he was pleased to find the assurance "RE TOM EVERYTHING OKAY."

That was jumping the gun slightly. Goins' trial was still scheduled. But when he next appeared in court—on September 15th, before Judge Neal P. Bottiglieri—he had nothing to fret about. Instead of a district attorney prosecuting him, here was Assistant D.A. O'Malley asking the Judge to have the case moved forward from the original trial date of October 5th, and, after the Judge assented, explaining in the next breath why the D.A.'s office thought the case should be dismissed. The Judge listened for a few minutes and then dismissed it.

"We must never become so busy that we can't afford to listen to a citizen," District Attorney Roberts said afterward. "We must never find ourselves too busy to rectify a wrong. We have to watch ourselves continually so we can give each and every person the treatment he deserves. But no human system is perfect. The truth usually emerges somewhere along the line, but sometimes things take too long. We have to figure out ways of accelerating our system of justice." A few days later, Kaplan found himself not too busy to write, on Goins' behalf, to the Messrs. Brewer, McGuire, and Kavanaugh, and Lieutenant Dwyer, thanking them for their "most exemplary help" and calling it "a rare but wonderful experience in this day and age."

Goins is paying his legal costs by having Grewcock take weekly deductions from his wages—a kind of extra Social Security tax. The chauffeur may someday get his money back, and more; Kaplan has filed a ten-thousand-dollar damage suit for him against the City of New York. That may take a couple of years to settle. Meanwhile, the lawyer has been trying to have Goins' arrest expunged from the municipal records—for a starter, to have his mug shots and fingerprints returned by the police. (But who can say for sure who may keep a copy? And, in any event, information about city arrests is routinely transmitted to the State Police and to the F.B.I., who don't necessarily return things.) Meanwhile, too, the Police Department conducted its own investigation of the incident. Assistant Chief Inspector Sydney C. Cooper, who commands all uniformed policemen in the Bronx, took charge. Little new evidence was turned up; in nearly every detail, Goins' story was confirmed. What, if anything, will happen to Patrolman Dengler will depend on the outcome of a Departmental hearing. Chief Cooper thinks the whole business may have been just one error compounded on another—a bad arrest, sloppy staff work in the precinct house, nobody's taking the time to listen to anybody else. "Do we have to pass laws and make rules before one person takes an interest in another?" Cooper asks. "Depersonalization is the crime of our time. Maybe it's not really a question of whether a patrolman violated Department regulations. Maybe it's a question, rather, of just not being humane."

Grewcock returned from Asia on September 20th, and was glad to find order restored to his life: his chauffeur was waiting for him at the airport. As for Goins, he has singularly little rancor. "I can't help wondering when they pick up somebody who isn't employed by somebody like Mr. Grewcock what will happen to him," he says. "Maybe if I were that person I'd still be in jail. But, basically, my attitude toward the police hasn't changed. I believe in the government and in the system, and I don't think I'm weak enough for something like this to tear me down. A number of people have asked me whether I'd let myself get involved if I found another envelope like that. Well, my answer is that my parents raised me to do the right thing, and if anything like this ever did come up again I think I would do the same as I did before." Goins hasn't yet seen the girl who stood him up on August 20th, but he says he has forgiven her, too.

HOW MEXICAN-AMERICANS VIEW THE LAW [4]

It was nearly midnight, and the barrio strangely quiet, quiet with fear. I had just left the Carioca restaurant with a dozen *tortillas de maíz* in a paper bag. I was spending the night before the funeral at my mother's house, and she'd promised to cook my favorite breakfast of *menudo con chile*. The tortillas, naturally, were essential.

Suddenly a police car screeched to a stop at the curb. Two cops jumped out and pushed me against the wall, frisking me from top to bottom with rough insolent hands. They said not a word, and neither did I. I was simply not *macho* enough to protest. A cop like these had blasted the skull of my friend Ruben Salazar, the Chicano columnist for the Los Angeles *Times*, in the Silver Dollar café and I was frankly afraid to cross them.

They have also arrested about 300 Chicanos since the police riot that erupted during the East Los Angeles peace rally that Ruben was covering on the afternoon he was killed. I didn't want to be "prisoner 301"—and, having flown all the way from New York, I certainly didn't want to miss Ruben's funeral. So I accepted the indignity of their frisk with a gut-souring meekness. This is all familiar stuff to anyone who has lived in a Chicano barrio. . . .

Suddenly noticing the brown paper bag in my hand, one of these guardians of the peace grabbed it and quickly shuffled through the tortillas in an apparent search for marijuana or heroin. Finding none, he gave them back. Later on

[4] From "Overkill at 'The Silver Dollar,'" by Enrique Hank Lopez, international lawyer, writer, and novelist. *Nation*. 211:365-8. O. 19, '70. Reprinted by permission.

I threw the tortillas into a trash can—they must have had a hundred cop fingerprints on them.

They let me go finally—a tribute to my meekness, to what I would rather call my old barrio wisdom. The pragmatism of fear. And in my confusion and resentment (or was it again a sense of prudent resignation?), I had not noticed their badge numbers. Nor would I be able to recognize their faces again. I'm afraid all cops' faces have begun to look alike to me. And that's tragic, in a way, because two years ago I wrote to Mayor Lindsay and the New York Police Commissioner, commending a police officer who had been extremely kind (fatherly kind) to my ten-year-old daughter when she was injured near our apartment while we were away, the baby sitter having gone astray. He had taken her to a hospital and stayed by her side for five hours. So it's not in me to be a cop hater.

Just below Soto and Brooklyn Avenue, while searching vainly for a cab on those deserted streets, I saw a police helicopter swishing over me like a giant insect, its bright, harsh searchlights probing the dark alleys and back yards of the barrio.

The Issue of Police Brutality

I wondered then if the police regard us Mexican-Americans as a community of barricaded criminals. The phrase came easily at that moment because that very afternoon the [Los Angeles] *Times* had quoted an expert as saying that the kind of missile that killed Ruben "should be used only against a barricaded criminal." Gene Pember, a consultant for the Peace Officers Standards and Training Commission, had told newsmen that the high-velocity tear-gas projectile that pierced Ruben's skull should never be used for crowd control, that "the thing is like a young cannon, really." Such missiles, he said, could go through a thick stucco wall. "That's what they are for—to penetrate a house or an object behind which a dangerous suspect has barricaded himself. But even then they should never be fired at a person." ...

Small wonder that my fellow Chicanos are willing to be-lieve almost any accusation against the police. When the *Times* subsequently devoted its entire front page to blown-up photos from a community newspaper called *La Raza,* quoting at length from an article titled "The Murder of Ruben Salazar"—they may have begun to entertain even that suspicion.

Earlier that evening (several hours before the cops frisked me) I had attended a rally of Chicanos at the All Nations auditorium, where I heard their collective rage and frustration—my own as well—burst from the throats of one speaker after another, the packed listeners periodically stamping their feet and raising clenched fists as a symbol of "Chicano Power." . . .

After the rally I went to the Carioca bar-restaurant to eat Mexican food. It was also a sentimental gesture. The last time I had seen Ruben Salazar we had come to this restaurant, mostly to hear the mariachi trio that entertains here. . . .

I told Ruben of my first encounter with the juvenile court system as a lawyer (I'd had several as a child). A Mexican-American woman had called my office in a state verging on hysteria. Her thirteen-year-old son—let's call him Ramon Gomez—had been picked up by the police and whisked off in a squad car, but no one at the local precinct station would tell her where he was. Within half an hour we were at the Hollenbeck station in East Los Angeles, and were informed that Ramon wasn't there. No record of his arrest. Then we hurried to the Juvenile Detention Home, where the desk captain said there was no booking on a Ramon Gomez. But as we were leaving, a young Chicano trustee told us that a boy answering Ramon's description had been taken from the detention home to the Los Angeles General Hospital. "He had a bloody bandage on his face." Checking the prison ward at the hospital, we learned two hours later that he'd received treatment for a fractured nose and then been returned to the detention home.

When we tried to see him at the so-called home, we were told he couldn't have visitors—nor could I see him in my capacity as his attorney. Angered by this refusal (any adult prisoner can see a lawyer), I went to a bail bondsman, who told me that kids weren't entitled to release on bail. Then I called several judges, who told me that they couldn't order his release on a writ of habeas corpus because children weren't entitled to that constitutional right.

When I finally saw the boy, he told me that he'd been accused of trying to break into a bubble-gum machine. "I put a penny in there and the gum didn't come out, so I was shaking it when the police came by. And when I tried to explain what happened, one of them slapped me. Then when I protested, they got me in the car, and one of them started punching my face with his closed fist, calling me a smart-aleck spick. That's how my nose got busted."

The Kafkaesque nightmare continued the next day at Ramon's hearing in juvenile court. The judge immediately informed me that I couldn't act as his lawyer "because this is not a criminal proceeding."

"Then why are you treating him like a criminal?" I asked. "Why has he been detained in that jail?"

"That's not a jail," he said rather testily. "It's only a detention home."

Paraphrasing Gertrude Stein, I said: "It has barred cells like a jail and barred gates to keep those kids inside, and a jail is a jail is a jail—no matter what name you give it."

But he still wouldn't let me appear as Ramon's lawyer, so his mother and I just sat there watching the nightmare proceedings of that quick-justice cafeteria called a "court." Not only were the juvenile defendants (almost all of them black or Chicano) denied lawyers; they couldn't face their accusers, they couldn't cross-examine witnesses against them, they couldn't object to rank hearsay testimony, they weren't protected by any of the normal rules of evidence. They were, in fact, unable to invoke any of the constitutional safeguards that are available to known gangsters.

And when I asked the judge for a transcript of the hearing after he had sentenced Ramon to six months in a reformatory, his mother pleaded with me not to appeal the case. "If we raise a big fuss," she said, "they'll only make it tougher on Ramon when he gets out. He'll be a marked man. We Chicanos don't have a chance." . . .

"The Fragile Society"

Ramon Gomez must be twenty years old by now. He may have been one of the tight-mouthed militants in the angry crowd at the All Nations auditorium on the night before Ruben's funeral, listening to one speaker comment on the tear-gassing of children at the peace rally. . . .

But quite aside from his own not-likely-to-be-forgotten experience with the law, Ramon knows about inferior ghetto schools with indifferent teachers, about poor substandard housing, about high unemployment in the barrio, about radio and television shows that demean and insult his fellow *paisanos*. And he must be aware that local and Federal Government agencies largely ignore the plight of 8 million invisible Mexican-Americans. And he certainly knows that the television networks, national magazines and news syndicates are generally deaf to the despairing voices of the barrio, although the more strident voices from black ghettos get ample notice.

Those same news media have been outraged by the alarming increase of cop killers—and it is well they should be, for any killing is abhorrent. But they should also know that the phrase is sometimes reversed in the ghetto—that Chicanos and blacks and poor whites often talk about killer cops with equal abhorrence.

Ramon and the rest of us Chicanos have been urged to turn a deaf ear to the dangerous cry of the militant, to listen instead to the voices of reason, to the voices of the people like Ruben Salazar. And though I myself felt slightly less than reasonable when those two cops shoved me against the wall on a dark lonely street, I would certainly agree that our only hope is reason and good will.

One must also hope that the police and other authorities will come to realize that reason flows both ways, that this fragile society can ill afford the frightening consequences of the kind of overkill that silenced the most reasonable voice of Ruben Salazar.

IV. BUT WHO WILL PROTECT SOCIETY?

EDITOR'S INTRODUCTION

In the American system of justice there is always some-one—trained and professional—who will speak for the accused. But who will speak for the victim of crime? Who will defend his rights and interests? The American system leaves this job to harried police officers and prosecutors; but even as many a victim lies nursing his wounds in a hospital bed, his assailant has often been released once more to the streets.

Lest the rights of the accused monopolize our attention, it is well to remember that society has its rights, too. The purpose of this section is basically to argue the case for "law and order," with all the implications that code phrase contains. More police, more courts, more laws, and more prisons —these are the things that the public has come to associate with law and order and that advocates of law and order enumerate as they build their case. More oppression of minorities, of the poor, and of political dissidents is how some opponents of the phrase tend to read it.

Perhaps the real meaning of law and order is best revealed in the article by James Mills, reprinted here from *Life* magazine. In his chronicle of a few days in the life of a leading defense attorney employed by the Legal Aid Society, Mills reveals with shocking clarity the moral bankruptcy into which the courts have fallen and the cynicism with which "justice" is being meted out. Like all first-rate reporting, Mills' account has that special ring of authenticity, and what it says about the current state of law and order in America should give anyone who reads it food for thought.

The other three articles in this section set forth official views on the law and order issue. In the first, the attorney general of Indiana attacks the permissive and lenient attitudes which, in his opinion, have helped make the victims of crime the forgotten people of this country. His sentiments are more or less echoed in the third article, which presents remarks to reporters by the President of the United States. In the final article, Deputy Attorney General Richard G. Kleindienst argues the case for pretrial detention as a means of assuring greater protection to society from criminal attack.

VICTIMS OF CRIME: THE FORGOTTEN PEOPLE? [1]

J. Edgar Hoover, the Director of the Federal Bureau of Investigation . . . has asked this question of all law enforcement officials: "Who speaks for the victims of crime in America?" And he gives this answer: "Aside from the weak, muffled cries of the victims themselves, practically no one."

And he goes on to say:

Are crime victims in the United States today the forgotten people of our time? Do they receive a full measure of justice? . . . While many victims are specifically picked by their criminal assailants, others are "chance" targets, ill-fated in being at the wrong place at the wrong time. No one is immune. As a rule, when criminal violence strikes, any number of things may happen to the victim. He may be murdered. If not, he may receive serious injuries, sustain a sizable monetary loss, miss time from work, incur costly medical and hospital expenses, and suffer untold mental anguish. To some degree at least, his right to freedom and the pursuit of happiness is violated.

Meanwhile, if his assailant is apprehended and charged, the full power of our judicial processes ensues to protect his constitutional rights. This is well and good.

But, how about the victim? Frequently, the compassion he may receive from the investigating enforcement officers, his family, and his friends is the only concern expressed in his behalf. Indeed, in some instances the crime victim witnesses organized campaigns of propaganda to build sympathy for his guilty assailant,

[1] From "Criminal Violence: How About the Victim?" address by Theodore L. Sendak, attorney general of Indiana, May 12, 1971. *Vital Speeches of the Day.* 37:574-6. Jl. 1, '71. Reprinted by permission.

campaigns of lies and innuendoes which charge that the criminal, not the victim or the law-abiding public, is the one who has been "sinned against." The tragedy is that in some instances these false claims are repeated and publicized without question by various means, apparently for no reason other than that those doing so want to believe the accusations. Consequently, the popular cause legally to protect the criminal is crowding his victim from beneath the dome of justice.

This introduction leads into an area that I think is of tremendous concern at the present time because of the near-sighted and one-dimensional drive by those people who don't think this matter through, or who have had no experience with the seamy side of human nature, and who are trying to paralyze what weapons are left to control the law-breakers and to guarantee the freedoms of all. . . .

Victims Don't Escape

Many criminals escape punishment; none of their victims ever do.

The public is treated to bales of propaganda to bring sympathy for murderers, but never a kind word for their victims.

For example, George Robert Brown was convicted fourteen years ago and sentenced to death for murdering Mildred Grigonis, a Gary beautician; Emmett O. Hashfield was convicted in Boonville in 1962 for the dismemberment slaying of Avril Terry; J. L. Dull was convicted in 1961 for the robbery slaying of taxi-cab driver James L. Tricker of Muncie; Luciano Monserrate was convicted in 1967 for the rape-slaying of Sharon Potts, a hospital clerk at East Chicago; Charles Adams was convicted in 1968 for the slaying of Burl Lyles of Huntington; Paul T. Kennedy was convicted in 1969 for the slaying of Porter County Deputy Sheriff Paul Blakely; Michael T. Callahan of Indianapolis was convicted for slaying Marion County Deputy Sheriff Edward Byrne in 1962. Duly tried and convicted, all seven murderers have thus far avoided their [death] penalties.

Every time the propaganda gushes forth to relieve these murderers and others of their punishment, it might be well if the press would give equal space to the story of the crime and the victim and pictures of the victim before and after the crime.

The purpose of our system of criminal law is to minimize the quantity of human suffering by maintaining a framework of order and peace. The primary object of the law in this area is to forestall acts of violence or other aggression by which one person inflicts harm on another. To the extent that government fails to do this, the primary function of the state is neglected, and individual suffering is increased.

The question we must ask ourselves about the death penalty is: Which of several possible courses of action will serve the true humanitarian purposes of the criminal law. We must weigh the execution of the convicted murderer against the loss of life of his victims and of the possible victims of other potential murderers. [For another view of the death penalty, see Section V.] . . .

The propaganda drive to abolish capital punishment appears to be a geared part of a general drive toward leniency in the treatment of criminals in our society. Such leniency has, in my opinion, had undeniable psychological impact on potential murderers, and has contributed to the upward spiral of the crime rate. There is a striking overall correlation between the recent decline in the use of the death penalty and the rise in violent crime. Such crime has increased by geometric proportions.

In the first three years of the last decade, the number of executions in the United States was by present standards relatively high. Fifty-six persons were executed in 1960; 42 in 1961; and 47 in 1962. During these same three years the number of people who died violently at the hands of criminals actually declined and the murder rate per 100,000 of population also declined.

Beginning in 1963, however, there was a drop in the number of legal executions, and the graph line of violent crime simultaneously began moving up instead of down. In the following years, the number of legal executions has decreased dramatically from one year to the next, until in 1968 there was none at all. But each of these years has seen murders increase sharply both in absolute numbers and as a percentage of population.

In 1964, for example, the number of legal executions dropped to 15. Yet the number of violent deaths moved up from 8,500 to 9,250, and the murder rate per 100,000 went up from 4.5 to 4.8. In 1965, the number of legal executions dropped to seven, while the number of violent deaths increased to 9,850, and the murder rate went to 5.1. Similar decreases in legal executions have occurred in the following years accompanied by similar increases in the murder rate.

In 1968, with no legal executions at all, the total number who died through criminal violence reached 13,650, while the murder rate climbed to 6.8 per 100,000.

The movement in these figures, with murders increasing as the deterrence of the death penalty diminished, confirms the verdict of ordinary logic: That a relaxation in the severity and certainty of punishment leads only to an increase in crime.

These remarks concern the deterrent effect of the death penalty on those who might commit murder but do not. That is a negative phenomenon which can be inferred both from the record and the assessment of common sense. The repeal of the death penalty would not repeal human nature. To these truisms we may add the fact that there are numerous cases on record in which criminals have escaped the capital penalty for previous murders and gone on to commit others.

Likewise there are numerous cases of prison inmates who have killed guards and other inmates, knowing that the worst punishment they could get would be continued tenancy in the same institution. Opponents of the death penalty usually resist even life sentences without parole, and the deterrent function of that would be even less effective than capital punishment.

The Results of Permissiveness

The general growth of violent crime in the past decade is the out-cropping of the attitude of permissiveness and leniency going hand-in-hand with an increase in the rate of victimization. As more and more loopholes have been devised for defendants, the crime rate has increased steeply. Between 1960 and 1968, the overall crime rate in America increased 11 times as fast as the rate of population growth —plainly meaning that more people are being subjected every day of every year to major personal crimes—murder, rape, assault, kidnapping, armed robbery, etc.

Is a course of action humanitarian which actually encourages a vast and continuing increase in the number of people killed and maimed and otherwise brutalized? There have been many sentimental journeys into the psychological realm of the criminals who are to be executed; I think there should be more sympathetic concern expressed for the thousands of innocent victims of those criminals.

Opponents of the death penalty may rejoice that in 1968 there were 47 fewer murderers executed in this country than was the case in 1962. But do they say anything of the fact that some 5,250 more innocent persons died by criminal violence in 1968 than was the case in 1962?

In the equation of human suffering, this is a staggering loss of more than 5,000 individual innocent lives. What about the human rights and civil rights of the individual victim? Are not those 5,000 persons entitled to the dignity and sacredness of life? Is that a result of which humanitarians can be proud? I think not.

Only misguided emotionalism, and not facts, disputes the truth that the death penalty is a deterrent to capital crime.

Individuals must be held responsible for their individual actions if a free society is to endure.

AN INSIDER'S VIEW OF JUSTICE IN THE COURTS [2]

Martin Erdmann thinks he might be antisocial. When he was six he liked to sneak across his family's red-carpeted, spiral-staircased entrance hall to the potted palm, and spit in it. At Yankee Stadium, he rooted for the Red Sox. When he went to Dartmouth, he cheered for Yale. He didn't make a lot of friends. He says he doesn't need them. Today he's fifty-seven years old, an unmarried millionaire lawyer, and he has defended more criminals than anyone else in the world. Because he is one of the five or ten best defense lawyers in New York, he gets those criminals turned back into the streets months or years earlier than they had any right to hope for. His clients are not Mafia bosses or bank embezzlers or suburban executives who've shot their wives. He defends killers, burglars, rapists, robbers—the men people mean when they talk about crime in the streets. Martin Erdmann's clients *are* crime in the streets.

In twenty-five years, Martin Erdmann has defended more than 100,000 criminals. He has saved them tens of thousands of years in prison and in those years they have robbed, raped, burglarized and murdered tens upon tens of thousands of people. The idea of having had a very personal and direct hand in all that mayhem strikes him as boring and irrelevant. "I have nothing to do with justice," he says. "Justice is not even part of the equation. If you say I have no moral reaction to what I do, you are right."

And *he* is right. As right as our adversary judicial system, as right as jury trials, as right as the presumption of innocence and the Fifth Amendment. If there is a fault in Erdmann's eagerness to free defendants, it is not with Erdmann himself, but with the system. Criminal law to the defense lawyer does not mean equity or fairness or proper punishment or vengeance. It means getting everything he can for his client. And in perhaps 98 percent of his cases, the clients

[2] From " 'I Have Nothing to Do With Justice,' " by James Mills, contributing editor. *Life*. 70:56-68. Mr. 12, '71. Reprinted by permission.

are guilty. Justice is a luxury enjoyed by the district attorney. He alone is sworn "to see that justice is done." The defense lawyer does not bask in the grandeur of any such noble oath. He finds himself most often working for the guilty and for a judicial system based upon the sound but paradoxical principle that the guilty must be freed to protect the innocent.

"I Like to Win"

And Erdmann does free them, as many as he possibly can. He works for the Legal Aid Society, a private organization with a city contract to represent the 179,000 indigent defendants who flood each year into New York City courtrooms. He heads the society's supreme court branch, has fifty-five lawyers working under him, makes $23,500 a year. Next to the millions left him by his father, a Wall Street bond broker, the money means nothing. Twenty-five years ago, until the accounting office told him he was messing up their books, he kept his paychecks stuffed in a desk drawer. In private practice he could have a six-figure income and, probably, the fame of Edward Bennett Williams, or F. Lee Bailey, or Percy Foreman. He is disgusted when people accuse him of dedication. "That's just plain nonsense. The one word that does *not* describe me is dedicated. I reserve that word for people who do something that requires sacrifice. I don't sacrifice anything. The only reason I'm any good is because I have an ego. I like to win.". . .

Martin Erdmann gets up at 4:45, reads till 6:30, then subways three miles downtown to the Criminal Court Building. He moves through dark, empty hallways to his office and unlocks the door. He is there at 7:30, two and a half hours before the courts open, and he is alone. In another ten or fifteen minutes Milton Adler will arrive, his boss, chief attorney in the criminal branch. Then, one or two at a time, come the phone operator and clerks, the other lawyers, the defendants on bail, mothers of men in jail, sick-looking junkies with vomit-stained shirts, frightened people who sit quietly on the seven wooden chairs along the wall, angry people mumbling viciously, insane people dressed in costumes with feathers in their hair.

Before the rush begins, Martin Erdmann sits at his desk in a side office and goes over the folders of the day's cases. Anthony Howard, a twenty-one-year-old Negro, is accused of using a stick and knife to rob a man of his wallet. Howard's mother visits him in jail, brings clean clothes and takes out his laundry. She doesn't know that the greatest danger to her son is not the robbery charge, but the man who sleeps above him in the eight-by-six-foot cell. Robert Phillips, Howard's cellmate, escaped from a state mental hospital seven years ago, was recaptured, released, then arrested for the murder of a twenty-two-year-old girl and an infant boy. After three more years in a mental hospital, he has been declared legally sane and is now awaiting trial for the murders. Erdmann looks over the file. "Prisoners who've been in mental hospitals," he says, "tell me they keep them there until they admit the charges against them. Then they mark them sane and send them down for pleading." He decides to give the Anthony Howard case to Alice Schlesinger, a young lawyer who can still believe her clients are innocent. She's good at what Erdmann calls "hand-holding," giving a defendant and his family more time than the case might need.

Milton Adler walks in and says something about a meeting he went to yesterday with D.A.s and judges to discuss ways of getting more prisoners out on bail. Erdmann listens and says nothing. What's left of his idealism, the wreckage, he defends against the day's events by affecting an air of playful cynicism. He smiles and laughs and pricks the pretty little bubbles of naïveté that rise around him from other lawyers. Listening to Adler, his face flashes now with the playful-cynic smile. "If they do reduce bail," he says, "it'll be the last they see of the defendants."

Alice Schlesinger appears in the doorway, a small young woman, about thirty, with long black hair. She wants to know what she can do to pressure the D.A. to start the trial

of a bailed defendant charged with robbery. "Can't we put
the screws to them a little? My client is very nervous and
upset. He wants to get the trial over with."

"Well," says Erdmann, "of course you can always make
a motion to dismiss for lack of prosecution. Say your client
is suffering great emotional stress at having this dreadfully
unjust accusation hanging over his head."

"Don't *smile* like that," she says. "He *is* innocent, this
time."

Erdmann gets rid of the smile.

Well, you know [he says], maybe the D.A. is having a little trouble
locating the complainant, and your defendant's on bail anyway,
so why urge them to go right out and track him down? Because
if they find the complainant and go to trial and if from some
extremely unfortunate occurrence your client should be convicted,
then he's going to jail and he'll be a lot worse off than just nervous.

She agrees reluctantly and leaves. Erdmann sits silently at
his desk, staring into the piles of papers. Then he says, "She
has a lot to learn. She'll learn. With some tears, but she'll
learn."

Why Trials Are Obsolete

Erdmann gathers up the folders and takes the elevator
to a courtroom on the thirteenth floor. He sits in one of the
soft upholstered chairs in the jury box and takes another
look at the thirty folders of the day's cases: a forgery, robberies (mostly muggings), burglaries, drug sales, assault
with a gun, arson, sodomy, an attempted murder. He ar-
ranges them on a shelf in front of the jury box and then sits
back to await the D.A.s and the judge. He is alone in the
courtroom, a dimly lighted, solemn place—meant to be imposing, it is only oppressive. Brown walls, brown tables,
brown church-pew seats soak up what little light the low-
watt overhead bulbs surrender.

A D.A. comes in and Erdmann asks him about a kidnapping case that's approaching trial. "The D.A. on that one's
on trial on another case, Marty. He won't be finished for a
month at least."

"Wonderful," Erdmann laughs. "I hope he stays on trial until the complainant's thirty. Then it won't look so bad. She was eight when it happened and she's already eleven." The D.A. shakes his head and walks away. Two more D.A.s arrive and Erdmann talks to them, joking with them, making gentle fun of them, establishing his presence: twice their age, more experienced, more knowledgeable, more cunning. "There's no question that my reputation is much too high," he says. "It's been carefully cultivated. Myths are very important in this business."

The judge enters: Mitchell Schweitzer, tall, thin, gray-haired, on the bench 26 years, 16 of them working closely with Erdmann. He flashes a look around the room, greeting private lawyers, Erdmann and two assistant D.A.s. [Since this article appeared, Judge Schweitzer resigned his post in the wake of charges of improper conduct.—Ed.]

The clerk calls a name: "José Santiago!"

Erdmann fumbles through his folders and pulls one out. "He's mine," he says. An assistant D.A. looks at the rows of folders on his table and picks one up. Erdmann and the D.A. walk slowly toward the judge's bench, pulling out papers as they go. Erdmann has, among other things, a copy of the complaint and a hand-written interview that another Legal Aid lawyer had earlier with the defendant. The D.A. has a synopsis of the grand jury testimony and a copy of the defendant's record. With these documents, in the next three or four minutes, while the defendant himself sits unaware in a detention pen beneath the courtroom, the judge, D.A. and Erdmann will determine the likelihood of guilt and the amount of time the man will serve.

Trials are obsolete. In New York City only one arrest in thousands ends in trial. The government no longer has time and money to afford the luxury of presuming innocence, nor the belief that the truest way of determining guilt is by jury trial. Today, in effect, the government says to each defendant, "If you will abandon your unsupportable claim of innocence, we will compensate you with a light sentence."

The defendant says, "How light?"—and the D.A., defense lawyer and judge are drawn together at the bench. The conference there is called "plea bargaining," and it proceeds as the playing of a game, with moves and countermoves, protocol, rules and ritual. Power is in the hands of the prisoners. For as increasing crime has pushed our judicial system to the crumbling edge of chaos and collapse, the defendant himself has emerged as the only man with a helping hand. The government needs guilty pleas to move the cases out of court, and the defendants are selling their guilty pleas for the only currency the government can offer—time. But no matter what sentence is finally agreed upon, the real outcome of this bargaining contest is never truly in doubt. The guilty always win. The innocent always lose.

To play the game well, a lawyer must be ruthless. He is working within, but *against* a system that has been battered to its knees. He must not hesitate to kick it when it's down, and to take every advantage of its weakness. No one is better at the game than Martin Erdmann.

Judge Schweitzer glances through the grand jury extract handed him by the D.A., a young bespectacled man named Jack Litman. Then the judge looks up over his glasses. "What are you looking for, Marty?"

How Plea Bargaining Works

Erdmann isn't sure yet. His client is accused of robbing a man on the street after stabbing him in the face, neck, chest, stomach and back. The victim was held from behind by an accomplice. "They have a big identification problem," Erdmann says. He is looking at a copy of a police report. "The DD-5 says the complaining witness refused to look at pictures in a hospital the next day because he said he wouldn't be able to identify the assailants from photographs."

"Your honor," Litman says, "they put sixty-five stitches in him."

"Just a minute," says the judge, and proceeds to read quickly to Erdmann from the grand jury extract: "They fled into an apartment house, the cop asked the super if he'd seen them, the super said they went into apartment 3-A, the cop went in, placed them under arrest and took them to the hospital where they were identified by the victim." He looks up. Erdmann has never heard the grand jury testimony before, and it hasn't exactly made his day. "So, you see, Marty, it's not such a bad case." He leans back. "I'll tell you what. A year with credit for time served." Santiago already has been in jail for 10 months. With time off for good behavior, that sentence will let him out today. Erdmann agrees. The D.A. nods and starts stuffing papers back into the folder. "Bring him up," he says.

Santiago's accomplice is brought in with him. Both men are twenty-one, short and defiant-looking. The accomplice, Jesus Rodriguez, has his own lawyer, who now joins Erdmann in agreeing to the sentence. The lawyers explain the offer to the defendants. They tell them that the offer can be made only if they are in fact guilty. Neither the judge nor the D.A. nor the lawyers themselves would permit an innocent man to plead guilty. Santiago and Rodriguez look bewildered. They say they are innocent, they did nothing. Much mumbling and consternation at the counsel table. Then Schweitzer says, "Would you like a second call?"

"Yes, your honor," says Erdmann. "A second call." The defendants are led out and downstairs to a detention pen. Erdmann looks at Santiago's interview sheet, a mimeographed form with blanks for name, age, address, education, employer, and then at the bottom, space for his version of what happened. Santiago's statement begins, "I am not guilty. I did nothing wrong." He has never been arrested before. He says he and Rodriguez were asleep in their apartment when the police charged in and grabbed them. At his arraignment some weeks ago, he pleaded not guilty.

"Talk to them," Judge Schweitzer suggests. Erdmann and his cocounsel walk over to the door of the pen. A court officer

opens it and they step from the court's dark, quiet brown-
ness into a bright, noisy, butt-littered hallway. The door
slams shut behind them. From somewhere below come voices
shouting, and the clang of cell doors closing. A guard yells,
"On the gate!" and precedes them down a dark stairway to
a barred steel door. An inside guard unlocks the door and
they walk into a yellow, men's-room-tiled corridor with windows on the left and a large bench-lined cell on the right.
Twenty men are in the cell, almost all of them dirty and
bearded, some young and frightened sitting alone on the
benches, others older, talking, standing, as at home here as
on a Harlem street corner. Suddenly the voices stop and the
prisoners, like animals expecting to be fed, turn their heads
toward Erdmann and his cocounsel. Three other lawyers
walk in, too, and in a moment the voices begin again—
prisoners and lawyers arguing with each other, explaining,
pleading, conning in the jailhouse jargon of pleas and sentences: "I can get you one and one running wild [two years
consecutive]. . . . I know a guy got an E and a flat [a Class
E felony with a year]. . . . So you want a bullet [a year]?
You'll take a bullet? . . ."

Erdmann walks to the far end of the cell and Santiago
meets him at the bars. Erdmann puts his toe on a cross strip
between the bars and balances Santiago's folder and papers
on his knee. He takes out a Lucky Strike, lights it and inhales.
Santiago watches, and then a sudden rush of words starts
violently from his mouth. Erdmann silences him. "First let
me find out what I have to know," he says calmly, "and
then you can talk as much as you want." Santiago is standing next to a chest-high, steel-plate partition. On the other
side of it, a toilet flushes. A few steps away, Rodriguez is
talking through the bars to his lawyer.

"If you didn't do anything wrong," Erdmann says to
Santiago, "then there's no point even discussing this. You'll
go to trial."

Santiago nods desperately. "I ain't done nothing! I was
asleep! I *never* been in trouble before." This is the first time

since his initial interview seven months ago that he has had a chance to tell his story to a lawyer, and he is frantic to get it all out. Erdmann cannot stop the torrent, and now he does not try.

I never been arrested [Santiago shouts], never been to jail, never been in *no* trouble, no trouble, *nothing.* We just asleep in the apartment and the police break in and grab us out of bed and take us, we ain't done nothing, I *never* been in trouble, I never saw this man before, and he says we did it. I don't even know what we did, and I been here ten months, I don't see no lawyer or nothing, I ain't had a shower in two months, we locked up twenty-four hours a day, I got no shave, no hot food, I ain't *never* been like this before, I can't stand it, I'm going to kill myself, I got to get out, I ain't—

Now Erdmann interrupts, icily calm, speaking very slowly, foot on the cross strip, drawing on his cigarette. "Well, it's very simple. Either you're guilty or you're not. If you're guilty of anything you can take the plea and they'll give you a year, and under the circumstances that's a very good plea and you ought to take it. If you're *not guilty*, you have to go to trial."

"I'm not guilty." He says it fast, nodding, sure of that.

"Then you should go to trial. But the jury is going to hear that the cop followed you into the building, the super sent him to apartment 3-A, he arrested you there, and the man identified you in the hospital. If they find you guilty, you might get fifteen years."

Santiago is unimpressed with all of that. "I'm innocent. I didn't do nothing. But I got to get out of here. I got to—"

"Well, if you *did* do anything and you are a little guilty, they'll give you time served and you'll walk."

That's more like it. "Today? I walk today?"

"If you are guilty of something and you take the plea."

"I'll take the plea. But I didn't do nothing."

"You can't take the plea unless you're guilty of something."

"I want the year. I'm innocent, but I'll take the year. I walk today if I take the year?"

The papers start to fall from Erdmann's knee and he grabs them and settles them back. "You walk if you take the plea, but no one's going to let you take the plea if you aren't guilty."

"But I didn't *do* nothing."

"Then you'll have to stay in and go to trial."

"When will that be?"

"In a couple of months. Maybe longer."

Santiago has a grip on the bars. "You mean if I'm guilty I get out today?"

"Yes." Someone is urinating on the other side of the partition.

"But if I'm innocent, I got to stay in?"

"That's right." The toilet flushes.

It's too much for Santiago. He lets go of the bars, takes a step back, shakes his head, turns around and comes quickly back to the bars. "But, *man—*"

He'll Take the Plea

Back upstairs at the bench, Erdmann says to Schweitzer, "He's got no record, your honor, and I've had no admission of guilt. You know I'm very careful with people who have no records—"

"And I am, too, Marty, you know that."

"He says he hasn't had a shower in two months, he's in a twenty-four-hour-a-day lockup, and he wants to get out, and I don't blame him."

"Marty, I'm not taking a guilty plea just because he wants a shower."

"Of course not."

"Do you want me to talk to them?"

"I think it might be a good idea, your honor."

Santiago and Rodriguez are brought up again and led into a small jury room adjoining the courtroom. Schweitzer reads the grand jury extract to the defendants, making sure they know the case against them.

Now Rodriguez says he'll take the plea. Schweitzer asks him to tell what happened the night of the robbery. Rodriguez says he and Santiago were on the street and they ran into the complainant and spoke with him and the complainant had a knife in his pocket and ended up getting cut, "but I didn't do nothing."

This departure from the original story, the admission that they had been with the victim and that there was indeed a knife, is enough for Erdmann. He looks at Schweitzer. "Now I'm convinced he's guilty." Schweitzer and Litman go back to court. Erdmann says to Santiago, "Do you want the plea?"

"Yes, man, I *told* you that, I got to get out—"

"Then the judge will ask you certain questions and you have to give the appropriate answers." He nods toward Rodriguez. "He held him and you stabbed him. Let's go."

They return to the courtroom and stand before the bench. Three times Schweitzer asks Santiago if he wants to change his plea, and three times Santiago refuses to answer. What if this is just a ruse to trick him into confessing? In exasperation Schweitzer gives up and moves on to Rodriguez. Rodriguez pleads guilty and is sentenced. Erdmann leans against the clerk's desk, his arms crossed over his chest, his eyes burning into Santiago. This ignorant, stupid, vicious kid has been offered a huge, heaping helping of the Erdmann talent, the experience, the knowledge, the *myth*—and has shoved it away. Erdmann's face is covered with disgust. Through his eyes, way beyond them, is fury—and unclouded, clear contempt.

The defendants are led from the courtroom. The clerk calls a case for a private lawyer, and Erdmann takes advantage of the break to get a cigarette. He goes into a small side room the court officers use for a lounge. The room has lockers, a desk, a refrigerator, toaster and hotplate—all of them old and beaten and scarred. Cops' jackets hang from the chair backs. Erdmann has forgotten Santiago. He stands by the window with his foot up on a radiator and looks across at the Tombs [the Manhattan House of Detention for Men], home of many of his clients, a desperate place of rats and rapes, beatings, murders and, so far this year, six suicides. Eighty percent of the 1,800 men in the Tombs are clients of the Legal Aid Society. . . . [In 1970] some of the prisoners, angry at the overcrowding, vermin and lack of official attention, decided to find out what could be accomplished by rioting. The riots were followed by avalanches of studies, committees, investigations and reports—some helpful, some hysterical.

"The Guilty Are Getting Great Breaks"

Erdmann is looking at workmen on a Tombs setback clearing away shattered glass and broken furniture from beneath burned-out windows.

It will never be the same [he says]. Once they've found out they can riot and take hostages, it will never be the same. Today defendants are telling the judges what sentences they'll take. I had a guy the other day who told me he knew the system was congested and that they needed guilty pleas, and he was willing to help by pleading guilty for eight months. The guilty are getting great breaks, but the innocent are put under tremendous pressure to take a plea and get out. The innocent suffer and the community suffers.

If the defendants *really* get together . . . [and] they all decide to plead not guilty, and keep on pleading not guilty, then what will happen? The offered pleas will get lower and lower—six months, three months. If that doesn't work, and they still plead not guilty, maybe the court will take fifteen or twenty and try them and give them the maximum sentences. And if *that* doesn't work—I don't know. I don't know. They have the power, and when they find out, you're in trouble. . . .

Forty minutes have been wasted with the stubborn Santiago, and now comes another problem. An Erdmann client named Richard Henderson says he was asleep in a Welfare

Department flophouse when another man "pounced" on him with a stick. The other man says he was trying to wake Henderson when Henderson "jumped up like a jack rabbit" and stabbed him in the chest. Henderson is charged with attempted murder.

Erdmann talks to him in the pen hallway just outside the courtroom door. It has started to rain. A casement window, opaque, with chicken wire between the plates, has been cranked open and cold air and rain are blowing in and making things miserable for Henderson. He's a twenty-one-year-old junkie—wire-thin, with deep, lost, wandering eyes, and a face sad and dead, as if all the muscles that could make it laugh or frown or show fear or anger had been cut. He stands there shivering in a dirty white shirt, no socks, no shoelaces, the backs of his shoes pushed in like slippers, hands stiff-armed down into the pockets of beltless khaki pants. Quietly, he tells Erdmann he wants to go to trial.

"Well you certainly have that right. But if you're guilty, I've spoken to the judge, and he'll give you a year with credit for time served. How long have you been in?" Erdmann turns the folder and looks at a date. "Six months. So with good behavior you'll have four left. It simply depends on whether you're guilty of anything or not."

Henderson nods. "Yes, that's why I want a jury trial."

"Why?"

"To find out if I'm innocent or not."

"Don't you know?" Erdmann takes another look in the folder. Henderson was psychiatrically examined at Bellevue Hospital and returned as legally sane.

"No, I don't know. But I have an opinion." His eyes leave Erdmann and begin to examine the hallway. He has withdrawn from the conversation. Erdmann watches him a moment, then brings him back.

"What is your opinion?"

"That I am."

"Well, if you go to trial, it may be four months anyway before you *get* a trial, and then you'll be gambling zero

against five or ten years. And even if you're acquitted, you'll
still have done the four months."

Henderson moves his feet and shivers. "I understand,"
he says meekly. "So I think I'd better do that."

"What?"

"Go to trial."

Erdmann just looks at him, not angry as he was with
Santiago, but questioningly, trying to figure him out.

"I think I'd better have a trial," Henderson says.

Erdmann leaves him and walks back into court. "Ready
for trial," he announces. "Don't even bother bringing him
out." Litman makes a note on his file and they move on to
another case.

Erdmann sits down in the jury box. The next few defendants have private lawyers, so he just waits there: watching, smiling, his bulging eyes gently ridiculing those around
him who have failed to see as clearly as he into the depths of
this charade, and to have found the joke there.

The judge is asking a defendant where he got the loaded
gun. "He found it," Erdmann whispers before the man
answers.

"I found it," the man says.

"Where?" asks the judge.

"Someone just gave it to him," Erdmann says.

"Someone walked by and handed it to me," says the
defendant.

Erdmann smiles. "It's amazing," he says, "how often
people rush by defendants and thrust things into their hands
—guns, watches, wallets, things like that." . . .

Giving Away the Courthouse

Guards bring in an old, toothless black man with wild
white hair and an endless record of rapes, assaults, sodomy
and armed robbery. He's accused of trying to rape a four-
year-old Puerto Rican girl. Some people driving in a car saw
the man sitting on a wall with the girl struggling in his lap,
and rescued her. Erdmann, [District Attorney Richie] Lowe

and Judge Schweitzer talk it over. Schweitzer suggests a year. Lowe [a young black man] runs his eyes again over the grand jury extract. He usually goes along with Schweitzer, but this time he balks. "I can't see it, your honor. I just can't see it."

Erdmann speaks a few urging words, but Lowe won't budge. "No," he says, "I just can't see it, your honor. If these people hadn't come by in the car and seen the girl, this could have been—it could have been anything."

Schweitzer, himself under great Appellate Division pressure to dispose of cases, now pressures Lowe, politely, gently. He points out that the girl was not injured.

"I just can't, your honor," Lowe says. "I just can't. This is abhorrent, this—"

Schweitzer breaks in. "It's abhorrent to *me*, too, and it's being discussed *only* in the light of the calendar."

"Your honor, we've been giving away the courthouse for the sake of the calendar. I can't do it. I won't do it." He stuffs his papers back in the folder. "Ready for trial, your honor."

He moves back to the prosecution table and announces for the record, "The people are ready for trial."

Erdmann has been saying nothing. As he passes Lowe's table on his way to the jury box, Lowe says, "Am I being unreasonable, Marty?"

Erdmann stops for a moment, very serious, and then shakes his head. "No, I don't think you are."

Lowe is upset. The next case has not yet been called. He moves around the table, fumbling folders. Then loudly he says, "Your honor, if he takes it *right now* I'll give him a year."

Erdmann talks to the defendant at the counsel table. Lowe keeps shaking his head. He is suffering. He takes a step toward the bench. "Your honor," he says desperately, "he should get zip to three, at *least*."

"I *know* he should," Schweitzer says.

Erdmann now stands and for the record makes the customary speech. "Your honor, the defendant at this time wishes to withdraw his plea of not guilty, previously entered, and plead guilty to the second count of the indictment, attempted assault in the second degree, a Class E felony, that plea to cover the entire indictment."

Now it's Lowe's turn to make the speech of acceptance for the people, to accept the Class E felony, the least serious type of felony in the penal code. He stands. "Your honor, the people respectfully recommend acceptance of this plea, feeling that it will provide the court with adequate scope for punishment—" He stops. The next words should be, "in the interest of justice." He sits down and pretends to write something on a folder. Then softly, as if hoping he might not be heard, he speaks down into the table: ". . . in the interest of justice."

He walks over to a visitor. "What do you think about *that?*" he demands. "That took a little *piece* out of me. He got a *year* for trying to rape a *four-year-old* girl."

Schweitzer recesses for lunch, and Lowe and Erdmann ride down in the elevator. Lowe is still upset. "What do I tell that girl's mother when she calls me and wants to know what happened to the man who tried to rape her daughter?" . . .

Law in the Afternoon

In the courthouse lobby after lunch, Erdmann stops to buy a candy bar. Someone says he saw a story in the *Times* that 5,000 of that brand had been recalled after rodent hair was found in some of them. Erdmann smiles and buys two more.

A court officer sees Erdmann coming down the hall. "Hey, Marty," he yells, "he's on the bench, he's starting to call your cases."

"So what do you want me to do," Erdmann says, "break into a run?"

Guards bring in a twenty-year-old girl charged with robbery with a knife. Erdmann is talking to her at the counsel table when Lowe strolls over and says, "Marty, an E and a flat?"

The girl looks at Lowe. "What's he saying, who's he?" Lowe starts away. "Don't listen to me, I'm the enemy."

She wants to know why she has to go to jail. "Well, rightly or wrongly," Erdmann tells her, "people think they shouldn't be robbed. So when they get robbed, they give a little time." She asks if the year can run concurrent with another sentence pending against her. Erdmann asks Lowe and he agrees. She still hesitates, and finally refuses the offer.

"What's wrong?" Lowe says. "She wanted a year, I gave her a year. She wanted it concurrent, I made it concurrent. It's unreal. They tell us what they want and we're supposed to genuflect."

"José Sanchez!" the clerk calls. A drug-sale case.

"Your honor, he hasn't been seen yet," Erdmann says.

"Let me see the file," Schweitzer says to Lowe.

"Your honor," Erdmann says, "he hasn't even been interviewed. I haven't seen him."

"Well, just let's look at it, Marty," the judge says. He goes over Lowe's file. "It's one sale, Marty. He doesn't have any robberies. Burglaries, petty larceny. Mostly drugs. I'll tell you what, Marty, I'll give him an E and a flat." Lowe agrees.

Erdmann walks into the pen hallway, and they bring up a defendant. "They're offering an E and a flat," Erdmann says to him. "For a single sale, that's about the—"

The defendant looks mystified. He says nothing. The guard interrupts. "This isn't Sanchez, Marty. It's Fernandez."

Erdmann drops his arms in disgust, and without a word he turns and goes back into court and sits down in the jury box. A defendant has in effect been tried, convicted and sentenced before his lawyer even knew what he looked like.

After court, Alice Schlesinger comes into Erdmann's office to brief him on a client of hers, a woman, who will be in Schweitzer's court tomorrow. "She's absolutely not guilty," Alice says. When she leaves, Erdmann's smile turns wistful and nostalgic. "It must be wonderful," he says, "to have an *absolute* sense of who's guilty and who isn't. I wish I had it."

Adler walks into the office. "What can I tell them?" he asks Erdmann.

Jack says he's leaving because the job's making a cynic of him. He says he thought he was going to defend the downtrodden and he finds out they're hostile and they lie to him. So he's leaving. Alice comes to me and says, "The system's wonderful for the guilty, but for the innocent it's awful. Some of them *must* be innocent." What do you *say* to that?

"You say nothing," Erdmann answers, "because it's true."

"No. You say that in a good system of government the vast majority get fair treatment, but there are bound to be a few who don't." He looks at Erdmann. "You think that's sentimental."

"I think you're a Pollyanna."

Adler turns to another man in the office. "He's called me sentimental, and he's called me a Pollyanna. And you know what? It's *true*."

Erdmann laughs. "What difference does *that* make?"

Serving the System

That night Erdmann goes home, has three Scotches on the rocks, meets a former judge for dinner, has a double Scotch, and thus fortified appears before the judge's evening seminar at the New York University Law School. Ten students are sitting in upholstered, stainless-steel swivel chairs in a red-carpeted conference room—all very new and rich and modern. Erdmann is supposed to tell them about jury selection and trial tactics, subjects on which he is a recognized master.

He unwraps a pack of cigarettes, lights up, and leans close over the table. Two of the students are girls. Most of the men are in jeans and long hair. Erdmann knows the look in their eyes. They think they will have innocent clients, they think they'll be serving their fellow man, the community, justice. They don't know that what they'll be serving is the system. He wants to give them some of the facts of life. "You are salesmen," he begins, "and you are selling a product that no one particularly wants to buy. You are selling a defendant who in all likelihood is guilty." They give him looks. "So you're going to disguise the product, wrap it in the folds of justice, and make it a symbol of justice. You have to convince the jurors that you're sincere, and that the product you are selling is not really this defendant, but justice. You must convince them that your defendant is not on trial. Justice is on trial."

The students are cautious. No one has taken any notes.

Your job is at the beginning and the end of the trial—the jury-picking and the summation. In between comes that ugly mess of evidence. In examining prospective jurors you have to sell your product before they get a look at him, before they hear the evidence. You want also to plant the seeds of your defense, and soften the blow of the prosecution's case. If you know that a cop is going to testify that the defendant stabbed the old lady eighty-nine times, you can't hide from it. You might just as well bring it out yourself, tell them that they're going to hear a police officer testify that the defendant stabbed the old lady eighty-nine times, and then when the testimony comes you will be spared the sudden in-drawing of breath. And maybe you can even leave the impression that the cop is lying.

A girl mentions the Tombs riots and asks Erdmann what could be done to give the prisoners speedy trials. During the riots, inmates' demands for less crowding, better food, extermination of rats and vermin were supported even by the hostage guards. But their demands for speedy trials, though they found strong support in the press, were less sincere. Virtually every prisoner in the Tombs is guilty, either of the crime charged or of some lesser but connected crime. He knows that he will either plead guilty or be convicted in a trial, and that he will serve time. He knows, too, that delays will help his case. Witnesses disappear, cops' memories fade, complainants lose their desire for vengeance. As prosecutors see their cases decaying, they lower and lower the pleas. Meanwhile, time served in the Tombs before sentencing counts as part of the sentence. Erdmann wants to explain that to the students, but he knows he will not find many believers.

"Let me disabuse you," he says, "of the idea that the prisoners in the Tombs want speedy trials. Most of them are guilty of something, and the *last* thing they want is a trial. They know that if every case could be tried within sixty days, the pleas of 1-to-3 [years] for armed robbery would be back up to 15-to-25."

"What about the defendants out on bail?" a student asks.

"People out on bail almost *never* have to go to trial. If you can get your client out on bail, he won't be tried for at least three years, if at all. The case will go from one D.A.'s back drawer to another's until it either dissolves into dust or the D.A. agrees to a plea of time served."

A student asks about the defense lawyer's responsibility to be honest. That triggers Erdmann's smile. "My *only* responsibility," he says, "is to my client. And not to suborn perjury, and not to lie personally. My client may lie as much as he wants."

Lost in Quicksand

So mired have the courts become that there now arises the nightmare possibility of a prisoner sinking forever out of sight in the quicksand of judicial chaos. In the postriot panic to relieve overcrowding in the Tombs, a special court was set up to facilitate the return to state prisons of inmates who had been brought to the Tombs to await hearings on various motions of appeal. One defendant entered the court in a rage. He was doing twenty-to-life at Sing Sing for stabbing someone to death with an umbrella. A year ago he was brought to New York for an appeal hearing. He never got the hearing, and went eleven months without seeing a lawyer. Finally in court—unsure as to when, if ever, he would reappear—he shouted furiously at the judge. Guards moved in around him.

The judge got things sorted out, scheduled the hearing for the following week, and the prisoner was removed. After a year in limbo in the Tombs, he had finally been found. The judge waited until the door closed behind the prisoner, then looked at Erdmann, at the D.A. and back at Erdmann. He said, "Now there's a man who's got a *beef*."

Since the case of Richard Henderson, the junkie who didn't know if he was guilty, was marked ready for trial, he has been returned each day to the detention pen beneath Schweitzer's courtroom—on the almost nonexistent chance that his lawyer, and the D.A. assigned to the case, and a judge and courtroom might all become simultaneously available for trial. Each day he sits there in the pen while upstairs in court his case is called and passed, with no more certain consequence than that he will be back again the next day, so that it can be called and passed once more. After several days of this, Erdmann speaks to him again to see if he has changed his mind. He is the same—same clothes, same dead expression, same mad insistence on trial. Erdmann tries to encourage him to take the plea, "if you are guilty of anything."

Henderson still wants a trial.

"What will happen today?" he asks.

"Nothing. They'll set another date for trial, and that date will mean about as much as any date they set, which is nothing. You'll just have to wait in line."

Henderson picks at some mosquito-bite-size scars on his arm. "The other prisoners intimidate me," he says. "They keep asking me about my case, what I did, what I'm in for."

"What do you say?"

"I don't answer them. I don't want to talk about it."

Henderson is adamant. Erdmann leaves him and goes back to court.

Erdmann's disrespect for judges (Schweitzer is a rare exception) is so strong and all-inclusive that it amounts at times to class hatred. When one of his young lawyers was held in contempt and fined $200, Erdmann left Schweitzer's court and rushed to the rescue. He argued with the judge and conned him into withdrawing the penalty. Then, outside the courtroom in the corridor, Erdmann's composure cracked. "He's a bully," he said angrily. "I'll put Tucker [one of his senior lawyers] in there a couple of days and tell him, 'No pleas.' That'll fix *that* wagon." He makes a note, then crumples it up. "No. I'll take it myself—and it'll be on the record this time." Erdmann remembers that two days earlier the judge's car was stolen in front of the courthouse. "I should have told him not to let the theft of his Cadillac upset him so much."

"There are so few trial judges who just judge," Erdmann says, "who rule on questions of law, and leave guilt or innocence to the jury. And Appellate Division judges aren't any better. They're the whores who became madams."

Would he like to be a judge?

"I would like to—just to see if I could be the kind of judge I think a judge should be. But the only way you can get it is to be in politics or buy it—and I don't even know the going price."

Erdmann is still in the hallway fuming over the contempt citation when a lawyer rushes up and says a defendant who has been in the Tombs five months for homicide has been offered time served and probation—and won't take it. Erdmann hurries to the courtroom. The defendant and his girl friend had been playing "hit and run," a ghetto game in which contestants take turns hitting each other with lead pipes. He said he was drunk when he played it and didn't know how hard he was hitting the girl. They both passed out and when he awoke the next morning she was dead. He had no previous record, and the judge is considering the extraordinarily light sentence agreed upon by the lawyer and D.A. Neither the judge nor the D.A. is in a mood for any further haggling from the defendant. Erdmann talks with the defendant and gets the plea quickly accepted. Five months for homicide. As he leaves the courtroom, a D.A. says, "Marty, you got away with murder."

Erdmann is gleeful. "I always get away with murder." ...

"It's Time People Were Told"

Every evening Martin Erdmann walks crosstown to a small French restaurant in the theatre district. He sits always at the same table in a rear corner, with his back to whatever other customers there are, and he is happiest when there are none. The owner and his wife are always pleased to see him, and when he does not come they call his apartment to see if everything is all right.

Not long ago he reluctantly agreed to allow a reporter to join him for dinner. The reporter asked him if he could be positive after twenty-five years that he had ever defended an innocent man.

"No. That you never know. It is much easier to know guilt than innocence. And anyway, it's much easier to defend a man if you know he's guilty. You don't have the responsibility of saving him from unjust punishment."

"What do you think about the courts today, the judicial system?"

"I think it's time people were told what's really going on. Everyone's so cowardly. Nobody wants to tell the public that the minimeasures proposed to clear up the mess *won't* do it. If you only had two roads going in and out of New York and someone said, 'What can we do about the traffic problem?' the answer would be, 'Nothing—until we get more roads.' You couldn't help it by tinkering around with the lights. Well, tinkering with the courts isn't going to help. We need more courts, more D.A.s, more Legal Aids, more judges—and it's going to cost a massive amount of money. I wonder how much money you could raise if you could guarantee safety from mugging and burglary and rape for $50 per person. Eight million people in New York? Could you get $20 million? And if you asked for $20 million to provide a workable system of criminal justice, how much would you get? People are more interested in their safety than in justice. They can pay for law and order, or they can be mugged."

"So what's the solution?"

"I've never really felt it was my problem. Everything up to now has benefited the defendant, and he's a member of the community, too. When you say, 'The people versus John Smith'—well, John Smith is part of the people, too. As a Legal Aid Lawyer, I don't think it's my problem to make things run smoothly so my clients will get longer sentences. That's the courts' problem."

He stops talking and thinks for a minute. Something is burning inside. "That's the wrong attitude, I suppose, but then the Appellate Division has never approached me and asked me what can be done to improve justice for the *accused*. They *never* ask *that* question. It's just how can we clear the calendars. It's how can we get these bastards in jail faster for longer. Not in those words—*certainly* not. They *never* in all these years asked, how can we have more justice for the defendants. That's why I'm not too concerned about the system." He has become angry and impassioned and now draws back. He concentrates on a lamb chop.

"I'm loquacious when I'm tired," he says.

After several minutes, he begins again. "You know, I really don't think there *is* any solution to the problem, any more than there is to the traffic problem. You do what you can within the problem."

"Is the day coming when the traffic won't move at all?"

"Yes. If every defendant refused to plead and demanded a trial, within a year the system would collapse. There would be three-year delays in reaching trial, prison riots, defendants would be paroled into the streets."

"What's Martin Erdmann going to do when that happens?"

"That's an interesting question. It would be too late by then to do anything. It's going to be too late very soon."

THE SYSTEM MUST BE PRESERVED [3]

We . . . wanted the opportunity to point out the fact that at a time that we are cutting budgets, that there is one area where we are drastically increasing budgets.

In this particular field, aid from the Federal Government to the states and to cities for law-enforcement administration rose from approximately $60 million in 1969, fiscal 1969, to $280 million in 1970, and this year's budget will be in the neighborhood of $450 million to $500 million.

We feel that this is the correct priority—the correct priority because the cost of crime to the country, not just in human terms but also in terms of the billions of dollars that the criminal elements take out of our society justifies this kind of investment, an investment not only in law enforcement but in crime prevention. . . .

But we do need a sense of urgency on the part of the Congress to pass more of the national legislation, to add to the District of Columbia bill that has already been passed, to deal with this problem: organized crime, narcotics, the whole area of pornography, and the rest. These are matters that are before the Congress. They deserve priority. And Congress should not treat this as a business-as-usual matter. This shouldn't be treated on a 9:00 to 5:00 basis. . . .

Glorifying Criminal Activity

As we look at the situation today, I think the main concern that I have is the attitudes that are created among many of our younger people and also perhaps older people as well, in which they [the news media] tend to glorify and to make heroes out of those who engage in criminal activities. This is not done intentionally by the press. It is not done intentionally by radio and television, I know. It is done perhaps because people want to read or see that kind of story.

[3] From remarks to reporters by President Richard M. Nixon, at the Federal Office Building, Denver, Colorado, August 3. 1970. *Weekly Compilation of Presidential Documents.* 6:1018-20. Ag. 10, '70.

I noted, for example, the coverage of the Charles Manson case when I was in Los Angeles, front page every day in the papers. It usually got a couple of minutes in the evening news. Here is a man who was guilty, directly or indirectly, of eight murders, without reason.*

Here is a man, yet, who, as far as the coverage was concerned, appeared to be rather a glamorous figure, a glamorous figure to the young people whom he had brought into his operations and, also, another thing that was noted was the fact that two lawyers in the case—two lawyers who were, as anyone who could read any of the stories could tell, who were guilty of the most outrageous, contemptuous action in the courtroom, and who were ordered to jail overnight by the judge, seem to be more the oppressed, and the judge seemed to be the villain.

Let us understand, all judges are not heroes. All policemen are not heroes. And all those charged with crime are not guilty. But let us well understand, too, that the system,

* The intent of the President's remarks was clarified by [White House Press Secretary] Ronald L. Ziegler in a subsequent briefing:

The President, in his remarks to you in this room earlier, was, of course, referring to the focus of attention and the dramatics that are oftentimes put on various criminal acts, alleged criminal acts.

Quite obviously, the President in his remarks regarding the trial now underway was referring to allegations that had been raised and are now in a court of law.

If you take the President's remarks in the context of what he was saying, there is no attempt to impute liability to any accused. The gist of his statement was just the contrary.

I think when he concluded his statement in reference to the system, in concluding his remarks to you, he made it very clear that it is important that in our system, as it does exist, that individuals have the right of fair trial, although, apparently, many of you understood it to mean something other than as the President intended it in his total remarks, to suggest that he was referring to something other than the obvious, and that is the fact that he was referring to the allegations against Mr. Manson and the others on trial in Los Angeles.

the system in which we protect the rights of the innocent, in which the guilty man receives a fair trial and gets the best possible defense, that system must be preserved.

And unless we stand up for the system, unless we see that order in the courtroom is respected, unless we quit glorifying those who deliberately disrupt, and unless we begin to recognize that when a judge necessarily, after intense provocation, must hold individuals in contempt of court, that judge is justified, that he is acting in our behalf, then the system will break down. The innocent will suffer, but more important, and just as important, I should say, the guilty will suffer as well because in a society without law, the guilty then have no trials....

But in the final analysis, unless the American people have within their hearts a respect for the system, the system of law and order and justice which we have inherited from over hundreds of years, then anything that we do at the governmental level will not be successful.

And it is that system that is now under attack in so many areas.

So we can be concerned about those charged with crime, we can be concerned about any evidences that those who are enforcing the law are going beyond their powers. But above all, let us remember that this system of law and order and justice must be preserved, and we must speak up for it. We must come to its defense and we must not consider that those—the judges, the police, and the others—who are simply doing their duty, that they are the villains and that those who are provoking them are always in the right.

Clarification of Remarks

[The White House Press Office later issued the following statement by the President prepared aboard Air Force One and given to reporters upon arrival at Andrews Air Force Base near Washington, D.C.:]

I've been informed that my comment in Denver regarding the Tate murder trial in Los Angeles may continue to be misunderstood despite the unequivocal statement made at the time by my Press Secretary.

My remarks were in the context of my expression of a tendency on the part of some to glamorize those identified with a crime.

The last thing I would do is prejudice the legal rights of any person, in any circumstances.

To set the record straight, I do not know and did not intend to speculate as to whether the Tate defendants are guilty, in fact, or not. All of the facts in the case have not yet been presented. The defendants should be presumed to be innocent at this stage of their trial.

THE CASE FOR PRETRIAL DETENTION [4]

Time and events have produced a crisis of disorder in American society. In the great cities of the nation, crime and its consequences press in on Americans, creating apprehension and fear, and seriously diminishing the enjoyment of life. As we examine the situation, nearly every form of criminal activity is on the rise, while the system we have developed for containing this lawlessness is breaking down.

"An accumulation of public neglect," as one observer puts it, has rendered the institutions of criminal justice almost incapable of meeting the present emergency. Nowhere is this more painfully obvious than in the nation's capital.

Crime's social turbulence is infinitely complex. A long view of things sees crime as the product of social forces, economic conditions, cultural patterns, and ebbing morals as much if not more than of human depravity. Recent studies have helped us to delineate with some precision the causes of crime. Among these certainly are:

[4] From address by Richard G. Kleindienst, Deputy Attorney General of the United States, before the American Trial Lawyers Association, Freeport, Grand Bahama Island, January 30, 1970. *Vital Speeches of the Day*. 36:354-9. Ap. 1, '70. Reprinted by permission.

The alienation, bitterness, and frustration of poverty, aggravated by racial tensions, in an urban setting;

The boredoms and stresses of great affluence as it coexists uneasily with conditions of poverty;

The steady dissolution of family life;

The rootlessness, confusion, and disorientation which result from urbanization and unparalleled mobility;

The fashionable permissiveness which condones misconduct; and

The growing disrespect for the sources of authority which help to regulate human behavior.

To these broad, sometimes intangible, and grimly persistent factors which contribute remorselessly to crime in society, we must add the present inadequacy of the criminal justice system. Fragmented in its operations and split in its perspective, the criminal justice system is failing to achieve its traditional objectives.

It is failing to deter criminals.

It is failing to restrain criminals.

It is failing to rehabilitate criminals.

And the failure of the system to achieve these objectives is generating an unfortunate but understandable spirit of retribution among an angry, fearful, and dissatisfied people.

The long-range solution to our *problems* with crime lies in a comprehensive effort to treat and remove the causes of crime—an effort involving the whole of government, in every department at every level. Such an effort will require a massive commitment of our energy and resources. It will require time. And we must remember that as long as the effort continues, it will compete with other national priorities of urgency and importance. Thus, the causes of crime, which we all agree must receive our most imaginative, dedicated, and intensive exertions, are not going to be eliminated within the life of this Administration or the length of this decade. Despite our best efforts and the expenditure of billions, these causes may still exist when the nation passes into a new century. . . .

We believe the alleviation of crime may be achieved, with relative speed and lasting effect, by reforming and improving the administration of criminal justice. This will take some modification in substantive law. It will take some revision of criminal procedure. But mostly it will require ample funding for police, prosecutors, public defenders, bail agencies, courts, correctional facilities, treatment centers, and the other institutions of the criminal justice system. To make this system work in the present crisis, we cannot give it less than generous support. We will pay for petty economies in blood and suffering. . . .

How to Reduce the Crime Rate

The crime rate will be reduced, at least to some extent, if we have police forces with the manpower and wherewithal to be present in the streets to deter and solve crime. As things stand now, the police solution rate for reported robberies in Washington is less than 20 percent. That feeble percentage will not deter crime. An expanded police force, well trained, well equipped, and sensitive to the issues of the day, can improve that statistic. The risk of apprehension which attends every crime must be increased.

The crime rate will be reduced when the offenders who are apprehended are processed without delay. When nine to twelve months elapse between arrest and trial because of choked and crowded courts, swift, sure justice is an idle pipedream. Crime will not be deterred by protracted proceedings; it will not be deterred by backlogs and delays. The court reorganization proposed by the Administration for Washington is prompted in large part by the necessity of removing these scandals from the system to speed the disposition of a criminal case.

The crime rate will also be reduced when sentencing practices once again reflect the objective of deterrence as well as the objective of rehabilitation. When a potential offender believes he will "get off easy" if he is caught, he will not be deterred from committing a crime. . . .

This determination to restore deterrence to the system must be matched by an equal determination to effect rehabilitation in correctional institutions across America. President Nixon has said that "no realistic program to substantially reduce crime can ignore the appalling deficiencies of our prisons and rehabilitative efforts."

At least 40 percent of all offenders released from custody eventually return to prison. The percentage of released offenders who commit new crimes is probably much higher. Recognizing this, the President has directed the Attorney General to formulate a ten-year program for a complete modernization of the physical plants and correctional programs in the Federal prison system, with the goal of developing model facilities and programs which state and local systems can follow. . . .

On January 31st of last year [1969], President Nixon asked Congress to amend the Bail Reform Act of 1966 to authorize the limited pretrial detention of dangerous defendants. The President observed that "increasing numbers of crimes are being committed by persons already indicted for earlier crimes, but free on pretrial release. Many [defendants] are being arrested two, three, even seven times for new offenses while awaiting trials." Thus, the President proposed that the Bail Reform Act be amended so that dangerous hard-core recidivists could be held in temporary pretrial custody when they are charged with a serious crime and when their pretrial release would present a clear danger to the community. . . .

Why Pretrial Detention?

The pretrial detention we propose is designed to accomplish two objectives. First, it is an effort to reduce violent crime, a significant percentage of which may be attributed to persons released prior to trial. Although pretrial detention would be authorized in all Federal courts, it would have its largest impact in the District of Columbia, where the problems of crime are by far the most serious.

Our second objective is to eliminate from the bail system the hypocrisy of locking up defendants, without fixed standards, through the device of requiring a high money bond. This second objective, of removing the shameful practice of detaining defendants arbitrarily by setting a bond which they cannot meet, is too often overlooked when considering this question. Let me discuss these objectives in turn.

1. Pretrial detention of selected defendants, in categories of offenses characterized by violence, is made necessary by the indisputable fact that many defendants are committing additional crimes during the period of their pretrial release. Precise statistics on the number of these crimes are not available because, until recently, no attempt was made to tabulate the incidence of crime on bail. Also, accurate statistics are simply not possible when many crimes go unreported and most crimes remain unsolved.

Nonetheless, the statistics we have are quite revealing. During the period between July 1966 and June 1967, 35 percent of the defendants indicted for robbery and released prior to trial in the District of Columbia were reindicted for subsequent felonies. In 1968, when 557 persons were indicted for robbery, nearly 70 percent of those released prior to trial were rearrested and charged with a subsequent offense.

Who are the people who commit these crimes? Some are desperate narcotics addicts with an irresistible need to support their habits. Some are incorrigibles, with long records of antisocial violence. Some have families whom they seek to "bankroll." Some commit crimes to pay a bondsman or an attorney. And some are out for a "last fling." Common sense tells us that while speeding up the trial process—which is the heart and soul of our court reorganization—will probably reduce the volume of offenses, none of the defendants here described will be particularly motivated to obey the law during the period of pretrial release. In the fifty to sixty days between arrest and trial—which is probably the minimum for serious offenses—the addict's habit will not disappear; the lifelong incorrigible will not be reformed; and the last fling phenomenon will still be present. Instead of spacing their crimes over a long period of time, many of these defendants can be expected to accelerate their misconduct, becoming more reckless and more dangerous because their time for planning action has been reduced.

To protect the public, we would retain in custody the most dangerous of these defendants, but only after a full-scale adversary hearing in which the court determines, in written findings, that *no condition or combination of conditions of release will reasonably assure the safety of the community.* The government's burden at such a hearing is two-fold: to show by a "substantial probability" that the defendant in fact committed the violent crime with which he is charged, and to convince the court that the defendant presently constitutes a danger to the community. If this burden is not met, the defendant will not be detained.

Under the standards thus established, there is no alternative to the detention we propose except a release which threatens the public safety. There is no alternative to the detention we propose except a rejection of the purpose of the criminal law.

2. Our second objective is based upon the fact that for centuries, courts have been detaining persons charged with crime by the simple expedient of setting high bond. This sham frequently served the purpose of protecting the community from dangerous defendants, but it also imprisoned people who posed no threat. When the issue of dangerousness silently appeared, there were not set standards or due process safeguards to protect the defendant under suspicion; and since there was no visible determination of dangerousness, there was little or nothing for a court to review.

This hypocritical procedure, which most often victimized the indigent defendant, was the evil to which the Bail Reform Act was directed. In place of money bail, the Act substituted personal bond and personal recognizance; financial conditions were to be imposed only when necessary to assure the defendant's presence at trial. In striving to eliminate

money as a barrier to release, the 1966 legislation was a great
leap forward, which more than justified its label of reform.
At the same time, however, by totally eliminating dangerousness as a criterion to be considered in setting conditions
for pretrial release, the Bail Reform Act ignored the ration-
ale behind seven hundred years of legal practice. Today,
Federal judges are faced with an agonizing decision when a
dangerous defendant stands before them. They must either
disregard the compelling mandate of the new law by setting
bail beyond the defendant's means, or they must shut their
eyes to community danger. One course perpetuates hypocrisy; the other course is reckless and irrational.

Ironies of the Bail Reform Act

There is a reason why the Bail Reform Act has not been
copied in the states. There is a reason why the money bail
system will continue to hang on. There is a reason why even
today almost 40 percent of some categories of defendants in
the nation's capital do not obtain their pretrial freedom.
The reason is that protecting the community from danger
is an imperative felt necessity of our law. By failing to meet
this necessity head-on, the defenders of the Bail Reform Act
are perpetuating a system of money bail which inevitably
discriminates against the poor. They are blocking needed
appropriations and authority to expand the District of Columbia Bail Agency so that many additional defendants can
be released on conditions prior to trial. And they are seriously jeopardizing the safety of the community, which is
powerless in some cases to prevent the release of a dangerous
offender.

Ironically, the Bail Reform Act is responsible for the
detention of hundreds of defendants who might be released
under new procedures. This Administration is prepared to
move vigorously to free these defendants, under some reasonable conditions, if they do not pose a threat to the community. But no movement in this direction is possible until
the law comes to grips with the dangerous defendant.

These issues are of critical importance when we relate them to vital trends in the law. For example, ten years from now, court decisions based on equal protection of the law may give the indigent defendant the means to force his release before trial if money is the barrier between jail and freedom. Such a development could not be welcomed by a society besieged with crime unless that society were empowered to protect itself against the truly dangerous defendant. That means of protection is pretrial detention. . . .

Balancing the interests of the individual and the public is a dilemma inherent in a free society. The questions are difficult for conscientious men. Today, as we reconcile the tensions between order and liberty, crime and fear weigh heavily in the balance. For they threaten important liberties as well as our lives. The time has come to face our responsibilities, to afford protection to all of our people. We can no longer neglect the security of our citizens. We must reassert *their* liberty to live without fear. Pretrial detention is not the whole answer; but it is part of the answer in this time of crisis.

V. OVERHAULING THE SYSTEM: WHAT CAN BE DONE?

EDITOR'S INTRODUCTION

Reforming the system of justice is an old and honored enterprise in the United States. The Constitution was barely established before Congress was elaborating on its article dealing with the judiciary. The process continues to this day. Despite the reforms—sometimes even because of them —things seem to have grown steadily worse rather than better. It is said that lawyers by and large are a conservative lot, and perhaps it is because of their past reluctance to invoke drastic change that the court system today is upon its knees.

But even lawyers are up in arms over the state of matters as they now stand. Some of them—younger, more dedicated to the public weal than to private practice—are even leading the fight for reform. And young or old, all seem to agree that the overhaul required will be costly. Chief Justice Warren E. Burger has put the cost factor in perspective by noting that "if there are to be higher costs, they will only be a small fraction, for example, of the $200 million cost of one C-5A airplane, since the entire cost of the Federal judicial system for one year, for the next year, is less than one of those planes. It is $128 million."

This section details some of the more important reforms in the American system of justice now going into effect and maps out the significant campaigns for further change. Following a brief historical survey of judicial reform efforts, Chief Justice Burger sets forth his views on the key steps that need to be taken to bring the present system back into balance, including improvements in Federal-state court relations. Next a writer in the *New Republic* explains why an expanded and politically independent system of legal services for the poor is essential both to the poorer communities it serves and to the general cause of reform.

The fourth and fifth articles of this section, taken from *U.S. News & World Report*, briefly recount some of the major changes in the administration of justice currently under way and the results of a four-year congressional study aimed at overhauling Federal criminal laws—most notably by abolishing the death penalty. There follows a brief editorial from *America* arguing provocatively that the right to a speedy trial—an issue that has aroused much concern and that has been commented upon elsewhere in this volume—is something of a false issue, since most persons accused of crime have every reason to applaud procrastination of their cases. It is suggested that more money for prosecutors, judges, jails, and prisons may be the answer, after all. In the last article, President Nixon places his own Administration squarely on the side of major reform and more money for the system, while exhorting all Americans to subject themselves to the rule of law: "We shall become a genuinely just society only by 'playing the game according to the rules'."

DEVELOPMENT OF JUDICIAL REFORM EFFORTS [1]

Trial delay appears to have been a problem in every organized civilization since the dawn of history. As early as the fifth century B.C., the judicial calendars of Greece were clogged. The British barons compelled King John to include in the Magna Carta the phrase "we will not delay justice to anyone." Shakespeare's Hamlet considered "the law's delay" to be as bad as "the pangs of mispriz'd love." The Sixth Amendment to the United States Constitution provided that in criminal cases "the accused shall enjoy the right to a speedy and public trial...."

The Constitution had relatively little to say about the organization of the American judiciary. Article 3 stated: "The judicial Power of the United States, shall be vested in

[1] From "Reform of the Courts," by Ralph C. Deans, staff writer. *Editorial Research Reports.* 1, no 21:412-17. Je. 3, '70. Reprinted by permission.

one supreme Court, and in such inferior Courts as the Congress may from time to time ordain and establish." The Founding Fathers were purposely vague about the nature of the court system because they were unable to agree on the need for lower Federal courts. The first Congress created such courts in the Judiciary Act of 1789 and they have been a part of the Federal court system ever since. That system today embraces eighty-nine district courts, eleven courts of appeal, one Court of Claims, and one Court of Customs and Patent Appeals. All are inferior to the Supreme Court.

Judicial reform in America is almost as old as the judiciary system. President John Adams declared in his annual message to Congress in 1799 that "a revision and amendment of the judiciary system is indispensably necessary." Congress finally heeded his plea when it passed the Judiciary Act of 1801. But what Adams described as reform, his Jeffersonian foes called dirty politics. Historians generally hold that Adams' motive in creating new judicial posts was to provide jobs for his fellow Federalists before Thomas Jefferson succeeded him as President. A number of judicial appointments —"midnight judges"—came on the eve of his departure from office.

However, there is another view—that judicial reform was actually needed. This view is buttressed by Adams' plea for reform before the Federalists lost the election of 1800. Regardless of which view is correct, the Federal judiciary became caught up in party politics in the early days of the republic and has never escaped that fate entirely—often to the detriment of genuine reform.

It is sometimes argued that when reforms are made, they arrive too late to do any good. Felix Frankfurter [noted jurist, associate justice of the United States Supreme Court, 1939-1962] and James M. Landis [noted lawyer and educator, dean of Harvard Law School, 1937-1946], writing in 1927, said necessary changes had been brought about "only after needs have gone unremedied for so long a time as to gather compelling momentum for action, or when some unusually dramatic litigation arouses widespread general interest."

Congress and Court Reform in Present Century

A problem of the early courts was the diversity of rules governing the judicial process. The Conformity Act of 1872 provided that the Federal courts should conform "as near as may be" to the practice currently in effect in the courts of the individual states. Since the practice of law varied widely from state to state, Federal courts were compelled to handle cases under a multiplicity of rules, many of them archaic and cumbersome. Congress in 1934 finally authorized the Supreme Court to adopt uniform rules for the Federal courts. These rules became effective in 1938 and are considered an outstanding example of court reform. State court systems still differ from the Federal system as to procedures of law, sentencing, the manner of appeal, and the method of selecting judges plus their terms of office and salaries.

To help clear congested calendars and to encourage uniformity in sentencing, Congress established the Judicial Conference of the United States in 1922. The body is composed of the Chief Justice as its presiding officer, the chief judge of each judicial circuit, the chief judge of the Court of Claims, the chief judge of the Court of Customs and Patent Appeals, and a district judge from each of the eleven judicial circuits. The Conference is authorized to survey the Federal judiciary, submit suggestions to the courts and recommend procedural changes to the Supreme Court. It is also empowered to recommend legislation to Congress. Until 1940, the Conference acted as the "benign housekeeper" of the Federal judicial system. Since then, however, it has gradually assumed a more activist role, commenting on legislation pending before Congress and making recommendations concerning the activities of Federal judges. Today, some members of the legal profession want the Conference to assume a disciplinary role over the conduct of judges. Others, fear-ing this would interfere with the traditional independence of the judiciary, want the body legislated out of existence.

Congress in 1967 created the Federal Judicial Center as an agency to improve judicial administration in the Federal courts. Chief Justice Warren told an interviewer that upon leaving the Supreme Court he wanted to help build up the Center. "The most important job of the courts today," Warren said, "is not to decide what the substantive law is, but to work out ways to move the cases along and relieve court congestion."

Roscoe Pound's Criticism of Adversary Justice

Pressure for fundamental reform in the legal system in the United States is often traced to a speech Roscoe Pound delivered to the American Bar Association in 1906. Pound, who later was recognized as an outstanding legal scholar, pointed out basic weaknesses in the judicial system. He criticized, among other things, selection of judges, overlapping court jurisdictions, and waste of "judge power" through inefficient procedures. Speaking out against the "sporting theory of justice," he said:

> . . . In America we take it as a matter of course that a judge should be a mere umpire, to pass upon objections and hold counsel to the rules of the game and that the parties should fight out their own game in their own way without judicial interference. . . . The idea that procedure must of necessity be wholly contentious disfigures our judicial administration at every point. It leads the most conscientious judge to feel that he is merely to decide the contest, as counsel presents it, according to the rules of the game, not to search independently for truth and justice.

Pound's criticism struck at the heart of the legal system in America—the idea that truth would emerge from making the defendant and the prosecutor adversaries. The adversary concept has often been criticized but is still a vital part of the judicial process of the United States. Pound believed the adversary system abetted "the modern American race to beat the law." "If the law is a mere game, neither the players who take part in it nor the public who witness it can be expected to yield to its spirit when their interests are served by evading it." His speech galvanized a spirit of reform. The American Bar Association created a Section of Judicial Administration in 1913. During the same year, the American Judicature Society was founded and began to investigate such things as the tenure and salary of judges, and court administration. More recently, it has advocated the selection of judges on a nonpartisan basis.

Many aspects of law that Pound attacked sixty-four years ago are still alive. His criticisms are echoed by reformers today. Lawyers are accused of trying to win cases, rather than have justice done. Francis Lee Bailey, the criminal trial lawyer, told the American Polygraph Association in 1968 that the courts were not interested in determining truth. "We're not separating the innocent from the guilty. We separate those against whom the evidence appears to weigh heavily from those against whom the evidence appears thin." Nor has criticism over the selection of judges died since Pound's time, as witness the Senate's refusal to confirm Supreme Court nominees G. Harrold Carswell and Clement F. Haynsworth. Their fitness for the Supreme Court was successfully challenged, in part because of their past rulings as Federal judges.

Search for Improved Ways of Selecting Judges

All Federal judges, including Supreme Court justices, are appointed by the President, subject to confirmation by the Senate, for tenure "during good behavior"—a term that means virtually for life since a Federal judge can be removed only by impeachment. To impeach a Federal official, the House of Representatives must bring formal charges against him for "treason, bribery, or other high crimes or misdemeanors" and the Senate, by a two-thirds vote, must convict him. Only four Federal judges have ever been so convicted. Thus it is almost impossible to remove a judge who is temperamentally, intellectually, or physically incapable of discharging his duties. Proposals have been put forward to empower Federal judges to remove a colleague for cause. There appears little likelihood, however, that this suggestion will receive practical consideration in the near future. For one thing, it would entail a change in the Constitution.

The tenure of judges of state courts ranges from life, in Massachusetts and Rhode Island, to four years in the major trial courts of many other states. Many legal scholars feel that both extremes are bad. It is often suggested that trial judges be selected for terms of not less than ten years, but that they be forced to retire at specified ages. The popular election of judges, a practice in many states, is widely criticized in legal circles. The idea of a judge on the hustings seems to run counter to the notion that the judiciary is "above politics." Yet voters of few states have been willing to change their constitutions to permit the appointment of judges. Some "good government" groups have advocated placing the name of the incumbent judge on the ballot, without opposition. Voters would vote "yes" or "no" as to whether he should remain in office. If the "no" votes carried, he would be removed from office and a new judge chosen and subjected to the same test of approval at regular intervals.

MAJOR STEPS THAT NEED TO BE TAKEN [2]

I would not be warranted in coming here today if I spent our very limited time reminding you what is good about our courts, or about the splendid and dedicated judges and others, most of whom are overworked to make the system function. I wish the public could know what the Association [the American Bar Association] has accomplished

[2] From address, "The State of the Federal Judiciary," delivered by Chief Justice Warren E. Burger, before the annual meeting of the American Bar Association, St. Louis, August 10, 1970. The author. Office of the Chief Justice. Supreme Court of the United States. Washington, D.C. 20543. '70. Reprinted by permission.

first in the support of public defender programs and now more recently in providing free legal services for people long unrepresented in civil matters. My responsibility today, however, is to say to you frankly—even bluntly—what I think is wrong with our judicial machinery and what can and must be done to correct it in order to make the system of justice fulfill its high purpose.

The changes and improvements we need are long overdue. They will call for a very great effort and they may cost money; but if there are to be higher costs they will still be a small fraction, for example, of the $200 million cost of the C-5A airplane since the entire cost of the Federal judicial system is $128 million annually. Military aircraft are obviously essential in this uncertain world, but surely adequate support for the Judicial Branch is also important.

Wall Street experts recently estimated that American citizens and businesses spend more than $2 billion a year on private security and crime control. Aside from the ominous implications of such private policing in a free society, just think what $2 billion could do for public programs to prevent crime and enforce law. That is where such support belongs.

More money and more judges alone is not the primary solution. Some of what is wrong is due to the failure to apply the techniques of modern business to the administration or management of the purely mechanical operation of the courts—of modern record keeping and systems planning for handling the movement of cases. Some is also due to antiquated, rigid procedures which not only permit delay but often encourage it.

I am confident that if additional costs arise in the process of making needed changes and improvements in the management of the judicial system, Congress will support the courts. But judges must demonstrate the needs clearly. Congress is harassed with demands for more appropriations for more and more new programs, each of which is labeled a high priority. We must first show Congress and the public that we are making the best possible use of what we already have and it is here that improved methods and skilled management techniques will count. These additions of equipment and personnel will cost relatively little in relation to the whole budget.

"Where the Action Is"

You know that in this brief report I can do no more than touch highlights and more detailed treatment of these problems must follow. I hope we can provoke debate—even controversy—to explore and test what I have to say. With increasing urgency every one of my distinguished predecessors from Chief Justices Taft and Hughes to Chief Justice Earl Warren have pressed these matters, but today I place this burden squarely on you, the leaders of the legal profession, in common with all judges. If the 144,000 lawyers you represent in 1,700 state and local bar associations will act promptly, you will prevent a grave deterioration in the work of the Federal courts. And you should remember Justice [Arthur T.] Vanderbilt's warning that these tasks are "not for the shortwinded."

In the Federal courts today the problem areas are essentially in large cities. Here we find in the judicial system no more than a reflection of the complexities created by population growth and the shift to large urban centers. The problems exist where the action is.

In Maine, for example, there is only one Federal district judge and literally not enough for him to do. As a result he has, for fifteen years or more, accepted assignments to go to courts all over the country where help was desperately needed. Many judges in the less busy districts have done the same. It is in the large centers that both civil and criminal cases are unreasonably delayed and it is there that the weaknesses of our judicial machinery show up.

How did this situation come about in the face of numerous additional judgeships added by Congress in the past thirty years?

When we look back, we can see three key factors:

First, the legal profession—lawyers and judges—did not act . . . to bring methods, machinery and personnel up to date.

Second, all the problems . . . have become far more serious by the increase in population from 76 million in 1900 to 205 million in 1970, and the growth of great cities and increase in the volume of cases.

Third, entirely new kinds of cases have been added because of economic and social changes, new laws passed by Congress and decisions of the courts. All this represents the inevitability of change and progress.

In this twentieth century, wars, social upheaval, and the inventiveness of Man have altered individual lives and society. The automobile, for example, did more than change the courting habits of American youth—it paved the continent with concrete and black top; it created the most mobile society on earth with all its dislocations; it led people from rural areas to crowd the unprepared cities. The same automobile that altered our society also maimed and killed more persons than all our wars combined and brought into the courts thousands of injury and death cases which did not exist in 1900. Today automobile cases are the largest single category of civil cases in the courts.

All this ferment of wars, mobility of people, congestion in the cities, and social changes produced dislocations and unrest that contributed to an enormous increase in the rate of crime. In a free society such as ours these social and economic upheavals tend to wind up on the doorsteps of the courts. Some of this is because of new laws and decisions and some because of a tendency that is unique to America to look to the courts to solve all problems.

From time to time Congress adds more judges but the total judicial organization never quite keeps up with the caseload. Two recent statutes alone added thousands of cases relating to commitment of narcotics addicts and the mentally ill. These additions came when civil rights cases, voting cases and prisoner petitions were expanding by the thousands.

Meanwhile criminal cases, once a stable figure in the Federal courts, were increasing. Added to that the records show that in all Federal district courts the time lapse in criminal cases from indictment to sentence has doubled.

Rising Tide of Cases

To illustrate some of the changes, consider just a few figures:

From 1940 to 1970:

- —Personal injury cases multiplied 5 times;
- —Petitions from state prisoners seeking Federal habeas corpus relief increased from 89 to over 12,000;
- —During this period Congress increased the number of judges by 70 percent, while the total number of cases filed in the Federal district courts nearly doubled.

But the increase in volume of cases is not by any means the whole story. Experienced district judges note that the actual trial of a criminal case now takes twice as long as it did ten years ago because of the closer scrutiny we now demand as to such things as confessions, identification witnesses, and evidence seized by the police, before depriving any person of his freedom. These changes represent a deliberate commitment on our part—some by judicial decision and some by legislation—to values higher than pure efficiency when we are dealing with human liberty. The impact of all the new factors—and they are many and complex—has been felt in both state and Federal courts.

The Criminal Justice Act of 1964 guaranteed a lawyer for criminal defendants—at public expense for the indigent

—and along with it appeals at public expense. The Bail Reform Act of 1966 authorized liberal release before trial without the conventional bail bond. Each of these Acts was an improvement on the existing system, but we can now see what was produced by their interaction in a period when crime was increasing at a startling rate. The impact was most noticeable in Washington, D.C., where Federal courts handle all felony cases. Defendants, whether guilty or innocent, are human; they love freedom and hate punishment. With a lawyer provided to secure release without the need for a conventional bail bond, most defendants, except in capital cases, are released pending trial. We should not be surprised that a defendant on bail exerts a heavy pressure on his court-appointed lawyer to postpone the trial as long as possible so as to remain free. These postponements—and sometimes there are a dozen or more—consume the time of judges and court staffs as well as of lawyers. Cases are calendared and reset time after time while witnesses and jurors spend endless hours just waiting.

If trials were promptly held and swiftly completed, and if appeals were heard without delay, this would be less a problem, and perhaps debates over preventive detention would subside. But these two Acts of Congress came in a period when other forces including decisions of the courts were making trials longer, appeals more frequent and retrials commonplace. We should not be surprised at delay when more and more defendants demand their undoubted constitutional right to trial by jury because we have provided them with lawyers and other needs at public expense; nor should we be surprised that most convicted persons seek a new trial when the appeal costs them nothing and when failure to take the appeal will cost them freedom. Being human a defendant plays out the line which society has cast him. Lawyers are competitive creatures and the adversary system encourages contention and often rewards delay; no lawyer wants to be called upon to defend the client's charge of incompetence for having failed to exploit all the procedural techniques which we have deliberately made available. Yet the most experienced defense lawyers know that the defendant's best interests may be served in most cases by disposing of the case on a guilty plea without trial.

A new category of case was added when it was decided that claims of state prisoners testing the validity of a state conviction were to be measured by Federal constitutional standards. As a result Federal district courts were obliged to review over 12,000 state prisoner petitions last year, as compared with 89 in 1940.

There is a solution for the large mass of state prisoner cases in Federal courts—12,000 in the current year. If the states will develop adequate postconviction procedures for their own state prisoners, this problem will largely disappear, and eliminate a major source of tension and irritation in state-Federal relations.

A Faulty Premise

There is another factor. It is elementary, historically and statistically, that systems of courts—the number of judges, prosecutors, and of courtrooms—has been based on the premise that approximately 90 percent of all defendants will plead guilty leaving only 10 percent, more or less, to be tried. That premise may no longer be a reliable yardstick of our needs. The consequence of what might seem on its face a small percentage change in the rate of guilty pleas can be tremendous. A reduction from 90 percent to 80 percent in guilty pleas requires the assignment of twice the judicial manpower and facilities—judges, court reporters, bailiffs, clerks, jurors and courtrooms. A reduction to 70 percent trebles this demand.

This was graphically illustrated in Washington, D.C., where the guilty plea rate dropped to 65 percent. As recently as 1950, 3 or 4 judges were able to handle all serious criminal cases. By 1968, 12 judges out of 15 in active service were assigned to the criminal calendar and could barely keep up. Fortunately few other Federal districts experienced such a drastic change, but to have this occur in the national capital, which ought to be a model for the nation and a showplace for the world, was little short of disaster.

Changes in the laws that are part of what we call the "revolution in criminal justice," which began as far back as the 1930s, have brought this about. Anyone who questions these changes must recognize that until the past two decades criminal justice was the neglected stepchild of the law.

There is a widespread public complaint reflected in the news media, in editorials and letters to the editor, that the present system of criminal justice does not deter criminal conduct. That is correct, so far as the crimes which trouble most Americans today. Whatever deterrent effect may have existed in the past has now virtually vanished as to such crimes.

If ever the law is to have genuine deterrent effect on the criminal conduct giving us immediate concern, we must make some drastic changes. The most simple and obvious remedy is to give the courts the manpower and tools—including the prosecutors and defense lawyers—to try criminal cases within sixty days after indictment and let us see what happens. I predict it would sharply reduce the crime rate.

Efficiency must never be the controlling test of criminal justice but the work of the courts can be efficient without jeopardizing basic safeguards. Indeed the delays in trials are often one of the gravest threats to individual rights. Both the accused and the public are entitled to a prompt trial.

The addition of sixty-one new Federal district judgeships by Congress within recent weeks is the result of efforts which began five years ago. Since it takes time to fill these important positions and new judges do not reach peak efficiency at once, their full impact will not be felt for a long time. We see therefore that the additional judges, needed in 1965, were not authorized until 1970. We cannot solve our problems by meeting needs five or more years after they arise. The time to plan for 1975 and 1980 needs is now, and I hope this can be accomplished, not simply by adding more judges, but by the more efficient use of judicial manpower and greater productivity through improved methods, machinery, management and trained administrative personnel.

Meanwhile, not a week passes without speeches in Congress and elsewhere and editorials demanding new laws—to control pollution, for example, and new laws allowing class actions by consumers to protect the public from greedy and unscrupulous producers and sellers. No one can quarrel with the needs, nor can we forget that large numbers of people have been without the protection which only the lawyers and courts can give.

The difficulty lies in our tendency to meet new and legitimate demands with new laws which are passed without adequate consideration of the consequences in terms of caseloads. This is dramatically illustrated in the current budget of the Office of Economic Opportunity. Congress has granted that program $58 million for legal services. That $58 million is a sound commitment to an underprotected segment of our people whose rights have suffered because they could not afford a lawyer. Few things rankle in the human breast like a sense of injustice. Whether the problem is large or small in the abstract it is very large to the person afflicted. We should applaud Congress for taking that step. But cases cannot always be settled by lawyers and the burden thus falls on the courts. This allowance for Office of Equal Opportunity legal services is almost half of what is allowed for the operation of all the courts in the Federal system. Here again we have an example of a sound program developed without adequate planning for its impact on the courts.

The Price of Deferred Maintenance

What this all adds up to is that for at least fifty years the Federal court system has experienced the combination of steadily increasing burdens while suffering deferred maintenance of the total judicial machinery—and added to that, much of the machinery has long been obsolete. The foresight of Congress in creating the Federal Judicial Center for research and study of court problems two years ago is one of the few bright spots in the past thirty years.

Now we must make a choice of priorities. When we want to dance we must provide the musicians and the public may well be called upon to pay something more for the Federal judicial system to increase its productivity. But neither costs nor the number of judges can be held down if the caseload is steadily enlarged.

To prepare for this report to you, I asked every Federal judge for suggestions. The hundreds of replies reflected a note of frustration and even anguish at the daily management and administrative burdens that drained time and energy from their primary duty to dispose of cases. That was the common denominator and the common complaint. Federal judges are today in somewhat the position of members of Congress a generation ago, before the Reorganization Act which gave adequate staffs to the Members and to the important committee work of the Congress.

The business of litigation is highly complex. To assemble all the necessary individuals is not as simple as TV shows depict. It actually involves the very difficult task of bringing together a judge, twenty-five or more prospective jurors, lawyers, witnesses, court reporters, bailiffs and others, at the same place at the same time without lost motion. The absence or tardiness of a single person will delay the entire process and waste untold time. Countless citizens serving as jurors have been irritated with the inefficiencies of the courts because they find themselves watching TV in the jurors' lounge rather than hearing cases in court. . . .

In basic principles, it is indeed essential that we maintain our links with the past and build carefully on those foundations because they are a result of thousands of years of human experience in the evolution of the law. There is great value in stability, predictability and continuity. But the procedures of the law ought to respond more swiftly—as hospitals and doctors, farmers and food distributors have changed their methods. Yet the major procedural change of this century was the development of the Federal Rules of Civil Procedure a generation ago. Except for those rules, Thomas Jefferson of Virginia, Alexander Hamilton of New York and John Adams of Massachusetts would need only a quick briefing on modern pleading and the pretrial procedures in order to step into a Federal court today and do very well indeed. We see, therefore, that the judicial processes for resolving cases and controversies have remained essentially static for 200 years. This is not necessarily bad, but when courts are not able to keep up with their work it suggests the need for a hard new look at our procedures.

If the picture I have been painting seems melancholy, I must in fairness touch on a few brighter sides—but sadly there are only a few.

In recent years the ferment stimulated by Roscoe Pound, [Arthur T.] Vanderbilt of New Jersey, [John J.] Parker of North Carolina—to name only three now gone—has brought on widespread growth of judicial seminars, institutes and study centers that have contributed much and we owe a great debt to my colleague, Justice Tom Clark, who has worked tirelessly on improvements in both state and Federal courts.

Perhaps one of the most significant developments in a generation is the creation this year—under the leadership of this Association along with the American Judicature Society and the Institute of Judicial Administration—of the Institute for Court Management at the University of Denver. Here for the first time is a place where court administrators can be trained just as hospital administrators have long been trained in schools of business administration.

Sadly even these bright spots emphasize how painfully slow we are to supply what courts need. The price we are now paying and will pay is partly because judges have been too timid and the bar has been too apathetic to make clear to the public and the Congress the needs of the courts. Apathy, more than opposition, has been the enemy, but I believe the days of apathy are past.

Tasks for the Future

As to the future I can do no more than emphasize that the Federal court system is for a limited purpose and lawyers, the Congress and the public must examine carefully each demand they make on that system. People speak glibly of putting all the problems of pollution, of crowded cities, of consumer class actions and others in the Federal courts. Some of these problems are local and we should look more to state courts familiar with local conditions.

Let me list some major steps for the future—steps to begin at once:

1. The friction in relations between state and Federal courts presents serious problems in both the review of state prisoner petitions and other cases. I strongly urge that in each state there be created a state-Federal Judicial Council to maintain continuing communication on all joint problems. Such a body could properly include a member of the highest state court, the chief judges of the larger state trial courts and the chief judges of the Federal district courts. In some states such bodies have already been created on an informal basis.

2. State and Federal judges should continue their cooperation with the American Bar Association to establish and maintain standards of conduct of lawyers and judges that will uphold public confidence in the integrity of the system we serve.

3. We should urgently consider a recommendation to Congress to create a Judiciary Council consisting of perhaps

six members, one third appointed by each of the three branches of government, to act as a coordinating body whose function it would be to report to the Congress, the President and the Judicial Conference on a wide range of matters affecting the judicial branch. This Council could (a) report to Congress the impact of proposed legislation likely to enlarge Federal jurisdiction; (b) analyze and report to Congress on studies made by the Judicial Conference and the Federal Judicial Center as to increase or decrease in caseloads of particular Federal districts; (c) study existing jurisdiction of Federal courts with special attention to proper allocation of judicial functions as between state and Federal courts; (d) develop and submit to Congress a proposal for creating temporary judgeships to meet urgent needs as they arise. Some state legislatures authorize such appointments based on a formula of population and caseloads in order to adjust promptly to population changes in rapidly developing areas; (e) study whether there is a present need for three-judge district courts and whether there is a present need for Federal courts to try automobile collision cases simply because of the coincidence that one driver, for example, lives in Kansas City, Kansas, and the other in Kansas City, Missouri; (f) continue study and examination of the structure of the Federal circuits that are now based largely on historical accident and are unrelated to the demands of modern judicial administration and management.

4. The entire structure of the administration of bankruptcy and receivership matters should be studied to evaluate whether they could be more efficiently administered in some other way. Pending studies on this problem should be pressed to conclusion.

5. Over the years various statutes and decisions of courts have altered many aspects of criminal procedure. Meanwhile some of the states have experimented with innovations and have developed new procedures to improve justice. Since Congress is now considering an entirely new Federal criminal

code we should soon undertake a comprehensive reexamination of the structure of criminal procedure to establish adequate guidelines reflecting adjustment to the new code, judicial holdings, and the experience of the states.

6. The system of criminal justice must be viewed as a process embracing every phase from crime prevention through the correctional system. We can no longer limit our responsibility to providing defense services for the judicial process, yet continue to be miserly with the needs of correctional institutions and probation and parole services.

7. The whole process of appeals must be reexamined. It is cumbersome and costly and it encourages delay and it takes too long. Some courts, notably the overworked 5th Circuit, have developed procedures to screen out frivolous appeals. Finality at some point is indispensable to any rational—and workable—judicial system.

8. We made a wise choice in guaranteeing a lawyer in every serious criminal case but we must now make certain that lawyers are adequately trained, and that the representation is on a high professional basis. It is *professional* representation we promise to give—nothing more—and always within accepted standards of conduct. This Association has now provided lawyers with comprehensive and authoritative standards and it is up to the courts and the bar of every state to make sure they are followed.

A Matter of Confidence

I have necessarily left some subjects untouched and others undeveloped but I hope I have imparted a sense of urgency on the problems and needs of the courts. I hope also I have made my point that it is not simply a matter of more judges but primarily better management, better methods and trained administrative personnel.

A sense of confidence in the courts is essential to maintain the fabric of ordered liberty for a free people and three things could destroy that confidence and do incalculable damage to society:

That people come to believe that inefficiency and delay will drain even a just judgment of its value;

That people who have long been exploited in the smaller transactions of daily life come to believe that courts cannot vindicate their legal rights from fraud and overreaching;

That people come to believe the Law—in the larger sense —cannot fulfill its primary function to protect them and their families in their homes, at their work, and on the public streets.

I have great confidence in our basic system and its foundations, in the dedicated judges and others in the judicial system, and in the lawyers of America. Continuity with change is the genius of the American system and both are essential to fulfill the promise of equal justice under law.

If we want to maintain these crucial values we must make some changes in our methods, our procedure and our machinery, and I ask your help to make sure this is done.

PROVIDING ADVOCATES FOR THE POOR [3]

Legal Services has been at once the most successful and controversial of the OEO [United States Office of Economic Opportunity] operations. A grassroots law and order program, it affords a means of resolving often explosive grievances among the poor for whom justice in court has so often been inaccessible. While the majority of the 1.2 million cases handled by its storefront lawyers over the past year were routine landlord-tenant, consumer fraud, social service or domestic relations matters, it has been the periodic test cases and law-reform activities that have caused political furor.

In 1967 California's [then] Senator [George] Murphy [Republican] at the behest of [Republican] Governor

[3] From "Advocates for the Poor: Legal Services, Inc.," by Ridgway M. Hall, Jr., an attorney in Stamford, Connecticut. *New Republic.* 164:24-5. My. 29, '71. Reprinted by permission of *The New Republic,* © 1971, Harrison-Blaine of New Jersey, Inc.

[Ronald] Reagan, tried unsuccessfully to prohibit suits against government agencies, and in 1969 the United States Senate passed a "Murphy Amendment" granting the governor of any state a veto over Legal Services programs. Immune from override by OEO, the veto would have deterred any poverty lawyer from bringing a politically controversial action on behalf of his client for fear of jeopardizing the entire Legal Services program in his state. The measure was defeated in the House only after a vigorous nationwide campaign by lawyers, bar associations, and client groups.

Last fall [1970] another battle was fought to prevent then OEO Director Donald Rumsfeld from carrying out his "regionalization" and "decentralization" plans, under which substantial control over policy and staffing of Legal Services programs was to be transferred from Washington to the more politically sensitive OEO regional directors. When regionalization was defeated, Rumsfeld fired Legal Services Director Terry Lenzner and his Deputy Director Frank Jones, both of whom had resisted the plan and have since become symbols of the poverty lawyers' commitment to clients.

Governors, mayors and other bureaucrats also have in some instances threatened to cut off funds and otherwise harass Legal Services. Governor Reagan annually vetoes the grant to California Rural Legal Assistance, which is widely regarded as the best in the country. Although in other years the veto has been overridden, this year the Nixon Administration responded by short-funding the program at a fraction of its former level for a six-month period pending investigation. In addition to posing serious ethical problems for lawyers, political interference in the attorney-client relationship has damaged morale in many offices, including the national OEO headquarters. A strong need exists to insulate Legal Services from political abuse.

The Mondale Bill

Senator Walter Mondale [Democrat, Minnesota] has introduced a bill to establish a National Legal Services Corporation, structured to provide such insulation. Modeled after the Corporation for Public Broadcasting, its management would be vested in a ten-member board of directors, five of whom would be chosen by the President with the advice and consent of the Senate. One would be appointed by the Chief Justice of the United States after consultation with the Judicial Conference of the United States. Six would be on the board by virtue of their office: the president and president-elect of the American Bar Association, the president of the National Legal Aid and Defender Association, and the presidents of the American Association of Law Schools, the American Trial Lawyers Association, and the National Bar Association. To assure representation of the views of clients and poverty lawyers themselves, three board members each would be selected by the newly created Clients Advisory Council and the Project Attorneys Advisory Council. The final member is the Corporation's executive director.

The corporation would have broad authority to provide legal assistance to low-income persons, and conduct related research, training and educational activities. This includes rule-making authority for such purposes as establishing eligibility standards, and guidelines for the conduct of the local programs. During a six-month transition period, all operations now performed by OEO Legal Services would be transferred to the new corporation.

Responsibility to Congress and the public is insured by the requirements of an annual independent audit, an annual report to Congress, the public availability of records pertinent to all grants and contracts, and the applicability of the Freedom of Information Act. At the same time, the Corporation is to operate free from political interference; no department or employee of the Federal Government is to have control over the Corporation or its grantees.

This bill would be improved by the addition of a provision ensuring that before a local program's funding is terminated it should be entitled to notice, a hearing, and due process of law. It is in complete reliance on Federal funding that such programs obtain and equip facilities and hire lawyers and staff, and it is usually disastrous for them if this funding is suddenly withdrawn.

The idea of transferring Legal Services to a corporation has broad support. The Mondale bill is cosponsored not only by such Democratic supporters of Legal Services as Senators Edmund Muskie [Maine] and Alan Cranston [California], but also by Republican Senators [Robert Taft, Ohio; Clifford Case, New Jersey; and Edward Brooke, Massachusetts]. Similar bills introduced in the House of Representatives also enjoy bipartisan support.

The White House approves the principle of incorporation but has its own bill, which is very different from Mondale's. It calls for: (1) a board of directors appointed by the President; and (2) major restrictions on law reform activities. The Administration's bill prohibits representation in criminal proceedings, prevents grants or contracts with law firms devoting 75 percent of their efforts to litigating in the public interest and forbids Legal Services lawyers from engaging in legislative activities except on request from the legislators. Lobbying on behalf of clients is restricted.

Instrument of Reform

Curtailing legislative activity by Legal Services lawyers, notwithstanding President Nixon's assurances to the contrary, would rob the program of an effective instrument for law reform. Frequently not only poverty groups, but state and local government officials have called upon Legal Services programs to draft or recommend legislation dealing with problems involving the poor, notably housing and welfare problems. This has produced some outstanding legislation. The restriction also runs afoul of Canon 8 of the Code of Professional Responsibility, which directs each lawyer to work for law reform through legislative and other means whenever he believes the need is there. Similarly as to lobbying, just as effective representation of a paying client may include lobbying, so should it be permitted in the case of a nonpaying client.

A ban on the use of public-interest law firms would be equally crippling, since the poor have many problems that can best be dealt with by such firms. Though the ban is expressed in terms of litigation, many lawyers believe it would also apply to firms conducting research which leads to litigation. This would cut the heart out of such organizations as the Urban Law Institute, the Columbia Center on Social Welfare Policy and Law, and the Harvard Center on Law and Education, which have been invaluable in pinpointing needed law reform and performing research which the Legal Services programs are not equipped to do.

Even under present law no Federal funds may be used for criminal cases, though funds from other sources may be. The Mondale bill would permit the Corporation to set its own policy on this issue, which seems preferable in view of the inadequacies of the present public defender system.

IMPROVING THE ADMINISTRATION OF JUSTICE [4]

Reprinted from *U.S. News & World Report*

At the Supreme Court in Washington, officials believe they can see the beginning of long-awaited advances in the way Federal-court judges operate.

Omens of the new era, according to these officials, include:

On December 12 [1970], the nation's first thirty men and one woman trained to serve as "court-management executives" were graduated from the recently created Institute for Court Management, a privately endowed school in Denver. They can serve in any court at the Federal, state or local level.

On December 23, Congress passed legislation allowing the eleven Federal circuit courts—the next step down

[4] From "Action to Help Clear Logjam in Courts." *U.S. News & World Report.* 70:65. Ja. 11, '71.

from the Supreme Court—to hire high-level administrators such as the new graduates of the Institute for Court Management. Their job will be speeding up and modernizing court operations.

The Supreme Court itself, high officials disclosed, will soon ask for an "executive" to improve the Court's internal administration. Congress will be asked to OK that innovation at a time when cases are pouring into the High Court at a rate of more than four thousand a year.

"Great Impact"

Chief Justice Warren E. Burger, in a year-end letter to all Federal judges, hailed the new "court executives" program as "a 'first' that may well have great impact on courts, law and the administration of justice." The Chief Justice has sought such a system since he took office in mid-1969.

While state and local courts are not directly affected, the new system may eventually lead to faster handling of appeals sent from those jurisdictions to the Federal courts.

Top officials of the Supreme Court say the "court executives" are the first major change in Federal-court administration in three decades. The last big advance was establishment of the Administrative Office of the United States Courts, which deals with the overall problems of administering the Federal-court system.

Under the December 23 law, each of the eleven circuit courts, representing the District of Columbia and ten regions of the country, will decide whether it needs one of the new administrators, or "circuit-court executives."

As of late December, only the circuit encompassing the New England states had indicated it does not need an executive at this time; and one other circuit court was not sure.

It will be primarily up to the chief judge of each circuit to decide on the executive's duties in that court.

A high official of the Supreme Court said this: "Truthfully, we don't know what those responsibilities will be."

But, essentially, he said, it will be the executive's job to relieve the chief judge of many of his administrative chores.

Up to now, the chief judge has been responsible for all administrative decisions of his court system.

At the same time, he has had to keep up with the staggering rise in the number of cases reaching circuit courts. In the past eight years, cases have more than doubled.

Supreme Court officials point out that in the Fifth Circuit, covering the entire southern part of the country—from Georgia through Texas—each of the fifteen judges wrote about one hundred opinions on cases last year.

The officials suggest that the first job for a new court executive in the Fifth Circuit might be to improve the way cases are screened before they are sent to the judges.

Other circuit courts are jammed with backlogs simply because the cases they are already handling have piled up —a condition officials suggest could be eliminated through better scheduling of cases by modern management methods.

One big hope: cutting the time lag in criminal cases. High Court officials said delay in criminal trials is the biggest single complaint they get from the public.

It will take some time to find enough of the right people to fill the new circuit-court posts, officials stress. They report fierce competition for initial graduates of the institute. More than two dozen states, as well as the Federal courts, are said to want this first group of specially trained persons.

One problem in filling the jobs: The law creating the posts laid down restrictions to keep them from becoming part of the political-patronage system.

Chief Justice Burger estimated in his letter to Federal judges that it may be late 1971 before enough qualified people are available to fill the circuit-court jobs, which pay up to $36,000 a year—only about $4,000 less than a United States district-court judge's salary. However, Mr. Burger is placing great faith in what they will be able to accomplish. He said:

"No other course offers any hope of bringing court operations into the twentieth century in terms of management that will match other developments in the law and the urgent needs of the courts.

REFORMING FEDERAL CRIMINAL LAW [5]

Reprinted from *U.S. News & World Report*

Sweeping changes in Federal criminal laws—including the abolition of the death penalty—have been recommended by a congressional commission after a four-year study.

If finally adopted by Congress, the proposed new Federal criminal code would constitute the first complete revision of substantive US criminal law in the nation's history.

The Commission on Reform of Federal Criminal Laws, which drew up the 317-page code, was headed by former Governor Edmund G. Brown [Democrat] of California, with Representative Richard H. Poff (Republican), of Virginia, as vice chairman. It was set up by Congress in 1966.

The major recommendations made in the report:

The death penalty could not be imposed in Federal-court trials. Only in the cases of intentional murder and treason could a life sentence be ordered.

A long list of major crimes generally considered punishable only under state law—such as murder, rape, arson and burglary—could be made Federal crimes when committed under certain circumstances. For example: When state lines are crossed, when interstate or foreign commerce is affected, or when the crime is committed in the course of another Federal offense. Legal authorities said this change would permit Federal prosecutions for murder when civil-rights workers are killed. Previously, Federal prosecution was permitted only for lesser offenses.

The Federal sentencing system—now with many dif-

[5] Article, "Death Penalty on the Way Out?" *U.S. News & World Report.* 70:55. Ja. 18, '71.

fering prison terms and a bewildering variety of fines—
would be simplified. Sentencing categories would be reduced to six basic types: Felony classes A, B and C; two
classes of misdemeanors, and a special category for minor
infractions deemed to be noncriminal. The three felony
classes carry maximum prison terms of, respectively, 30,
15 and 7 years. For the two types of misdemeanors, the
maximums would be 1 year and 30 days. Minor infractions would call only for fines.

Included in the Class A felonies would be murder,
treason, aggravated rape, kidnapping, espionage, sabotage and robbery—although murder and treason could
draw life sentences.

Broad Revisions Set

Other proposed changes:

Corporations. Companies found guilty of consumer
frauds and other illegal practices would face stiffer penalties.
Fines could be set at double the gain realized by the corporation, or double the losses to victims.

Judges could also require a guilty company to advertise
its transgression so that victims would be notified. Class
actions would be permitted for individuals to recover damages from corporations. Company or union officials found
responsible could be barred from holding similar offices for
up to five years.

Marijuana. The first conviction for possession of marijuana would be made a minor infraction—punishable only
by a fine. Harsher penalties would be provided for pushers
of narcotics.

Contempt. A maximum sentence of six months could be
imposed by a judge for summary contempt of court. A series
of contempt sentences could, generally, run to a total of no
longer than a year.

Firearms. Possession of handguns by private citizens
would be banned. Other firearms would have to be regis-

tered. It would be a Federal offense to use firearms in a riot. Engaging in paramilitary activities not authorized by law would be forbidden.

Taxes. Evasion of taxes would be a misdemeanor for small amounts and a felony for amounts over $25,000.

Defense pleas. The proposed code would spell out definitions of the more common defenses in order to do away with conflicting rules of Federal judges in different circuits. Included are such defenses as alibi, self-defense, insanity, intoxication and duress.

Sex offenses. Homosexual acts between consenting adults would not be considered crimes.

Paroles. Each sentence of six months or longer would consist of an imprisonment part and a parole part. The report noted: "This contrasts with present law under which a prisoner may serve out his sentence within the walls and emerge without parole supervision."

Crimes abroad. Federal prosecution of servicemen and United States citizens for crimes committed abroad would be permitted.

Any of these changes in existing law could be dropped or modified when the new code is taken up by Congress. Final action is expected to take several years.

One of the more controversial provisions is likely to be the abolition of capital punishment.

The death penalty has already been abolished in ten states, and restricted in four others. If the Federal Government should now outlaw capital punishment in Federal cases, other states could be expected to follow suit.

Before that happens, however, the death penalty might be abolished through another route: the United States Supreme Court. There have been no executions in the United States since June 1967. Prisoners facing that penalty await the outcome of Court cases challenging some death sentences.

THE ANSWER IS MORE MONEY [6]

Amid [1970] campaign cries for more law and order, prisoners in the New York City jails rioted against intolerable overcrowding, and public officials promptly conceded that the prisoners were right. After some half-hearted efforts at improving the conditions in the prisons, public discussions shifted to the problem of speeding up the criminal process so that the average amount of time spent by prisoners awaiting trial could be greatly reduced.

This was an unfortunate shift of emphasis. The right to a speedy trial is, indeed, a natural and constitutional right, but very few people choose to exercise it. Most persons charged with crimes plead guilty, either to the original or a lesser offense. Most of those who contest the charges want ample time to prepare for their defense and to take advantage of every procedural safeguard and technicality. Criminal defense lawyers, as a group, are among the greatest procrastinators in the world, and with good reason: they know that delay more often helps than hurts their clients. It is the rare defendant in a criminal case who really wants a speedy trial, and such defendants can be accommodated without major changes in our judicial system or substantial expenditures of money.

Paying the Price

It is, therefore, absurd to suggest that jails in New York and other major cities are overcrowded because judges and prosecutors are unwilling or unable to speed up the criminal process. The jails are overcrowded because Americans are unwilling to spend the money to provide decent jails for the people they want to keep in jail. Prison conditions throughout the country demonstrate that Americans are unwilling to pay the high cost of criminal laws. That is what makes the campaign cries for law and order so hollow.

[6] Editorial, "The High Cost of Criminal Laws." *America*. 123:310-11. O. 24, '70. Reprinted by permission. All rights reserved. © 1970. America Press, Inc. 106 W. 56th St. New York 10019.

We could solve the problem of overcrowding jails with defendants awaiting trial by abolishing detention before trial. But we are not willing to do that; in fact, we are seriously considering much wider use of "preventive detention." We could solve the problem of congested calendars in the criminal courts by abolishing most of our criminal laws that have nothing to do with violence, fraud or the protection of the young. But we are not willing to do that; in fact, we are seriously considering making a host of activities Federal as well as state crimes.

We cannot have it both ways. We cannot call for law and order and refuse to spend what it takes to restore law and order. We cannot call for criminal justice, and refuse to spend what it takes in the form of prosecutors, judges, jails and prisons. Criminals have to pay the price for breaking the law, but we have to pay the price for making it.

"HOLD FAST TO THE RIGHT ...
CHANGE THE WRONG" [7]

The purpose of this conference is "to improve the process of justice." We all know how urgent the need is for that improvement at both the state and Federal level. Interminable delays in civil cases, unconscionable delays in criminal cases, inconsistent and unfair bail impositions, a steadily growing backlog of work that threatens to make the delays worse tomorrow than they are today—and all this concerns everyone who wants to see justice done.

Overcrowded penal institutions, unremitting pressure on judges and prosecutors to process cases by plea bargaining, without the safeguards recently set forth by the American Bar Association, the clogging of court calendars with inappropriate or relatively unimportant matters—all this sends everyone in the system of justice home at night feeling as if he had been trying to brush back a flood with a broom.

[7] From address delivered by President Richard M. Nixon before the National Conference on the Judiciary, Williamsburg, Virginia, March 11, 1971. *Weekly Compilation of Presidential Documents.* 7:460-6. Mr. 15, '71.

Many hardworking, dedicated judges, lawyers, penologists, law enforcement officials are coming to this conclusion: that a system of criminal justice that can guarantee neither a speedy trial nor a safe community cannot excuse its failure by pointing to an elaborate system of safeguards for the accused. Justice dictates not only that the innocent man go free, but that the guilty be punished for his crimes.

When the average citizen comes into court as a party or a witness, and he sees that court bogged down and unable to function effectively, he wonders how this was permitted to happen. Who is to blame? Members of the bench and the bar are not alone responsible for the congestion of justice.

The nation has turned increasingly to the courts to cure deep-seated ills of our society—and the courts have responded; as a result, they have burdens unknown to the legal system a generation ago. In addition, the courts had to bear the brunt of the rise in crime—almost 150 percent over the past ten years, an explosion unparalleled in our history.

And now we see the courts being turned to, as they should be, to enter still more fields—from offenses against the environment to new facets of consumer protection and a fresh concern for small claimants. We know, too, that the court system has added to its own workload by enlarging the rights of the accused, providing more counsel in order to protect basic liberties.

More of the Same Is Not Enough

Our courts are overloaded for the best reasons: because our society found the courts willing—and partially able—to assume the burden of its gravest problems. Throughout a tumultuous generation, our system of justice has helped America improve itself; there is an urgent need now for America to help the courts improve our system of justice.

But if we limit ourselves to calling for more judges, more police, more lawyers operating in the same system, we will produce more backlogs, more delays, more litigation, more jails, and more criminals. "More of the same" is not the answer. What is needed now is genuine reform—the kind of change that requires imagination and daring, that demands a focus on ultimate goals, just as you have indicated imagination and daring and are focusing on ultimate goals.

The ultimate goal of changing the process of justice is not to put more people in jail or merely to provide a faster flow of litigation. It is to resolve conflict speedily but fairly, to reverse the trend toward crime and violence, to reinstill a respect for law in all of our people. . . .

The founders of this nation wrote these words into the Bill of Rights: "the accused shall enjoy the right to a speedy and public trial." The word *speedy* was nowhere modified or watered down in that Constitution or any time since by a court opinion. We have to assume they meant exactly what they said—a speedy trial.

It is not an impossible goal. In criminal cases in Great Britain today, most accused persons are brought to trial within sixty days after arrest. And most appeals in Britain are decided within three months after they are filed.

Let's look at the situation in the United States. In case after case, the delay between arrest and trial is far too long. In New York and Philadelphia, the delay is over 5 months; in the State of Ohio, it's over 6 months; in Chicago, an accused man waits 6 to 9 months before his case even comes up. . . .

Justice delayed is not only justice denied, it is also justice circumvented, justice mocked, the system of justice undermined.

Call for Use of Paraprofessionals

What can be done now to break the logjam of justice today, to ensure the right to a speedy trial—to enhance respect for law? We have to find ways to clear the courts of the endless streams of what are termed "victimless crimes" that get in the way of serious consideration of serious crimes. There are more important matters for highly skilled judges and prosecutors than minor traffic offenses, loitering, and drunkenness.

We should open our eyes—as the medical profession is doing—to the use of paraprofessionals in the law. Working under the supervision of trained attorneys, "parajudges" could deal with many of the essentially administrative matters of the law, freeing the judges to do what a judge only can do: and that is to judge. The development of the new office of magistrates in the Federal system is a step in that right direction. In addition, we should take advantage of many technical advances such as electronic information retrieval, to expedite the result in both new and traditional areas of the law.

But new efficiencies alone, important as they are, are not enough to reinstill respect in our system of justice. A courtroom must be a place where a fair balance must be struck between the rights of society and the rights of the individual.

We all know how the drama of a courtroom often lends itself to exploitation and, whether it is deliberate or inadvertent, such exploitation is something we all must be alert to prevent. All too often, the right of the accused to a fair trial is eroded by prejudicial publicity. We must never forget that a primary purpose underlying the defendant's right to a speedy and public trial is to prevent star-chamber proceedings and not to put on an exciting show or to satisfy public curiosity at the expense of the defendant.

And in this regard, if I may step into controversial territory for a moment, I strongly agree with the Chief Justice's view that the filming of judicial proceedings, or the introduction of live television to the courtroom, would be a mistake. The solemn business of justice cannot be subject to the command of "lights, camera, action."

The white light of publicity can be a cruel glare, often damaging to the innocent bystander thrust into it, and doubly damaging to the innocent victims of violence. Here again a balance must be struck: The right of a free press must be weighed carefully against an individual's right to privacy.

Sometimes, however, the shoe is on the other foot: Society must be protected from the exploitation of the courts by publicity seekers. Neither the rights of society nor the rights of the individual are being protected when a court tolerates anyone's abuse of the judicial process. When a court becomes a stage or the center ring of a circus, it ceases to be a court. The vast majority of Americans are grateful to those judges who insist on order in their courts and who will not be bullied or stampeded by those who hold in contempt all this nation's judicial system stands for.

Now, the reasons for safeguarding the dignity of the courtroom and clearing away the underbrush that delays the process of justice go far beyond the questions of taste and tradition. They go to the central issue confronting American justice today.

How can we answer the need for more and more effective access to the courts, for the resolution of large and small controversies, the protection of individual and community interests? The right to representation by counsel, the prompt disposition of cases—advocacy and adjudication—are fundamental rights that must be assured to all of our citizens.

In a society that cherishes change, in a society that enshrines diversity in its Constitution, in a system of justice that pits one adversary against another to find the truth, there is always going to be conflict. Taken to the street, conflict is a destructive force; taken to the courts, conflict can be a creative force.

What Is to Be Done?

What can be done to make certain that civil conflict is resolved in the peaceful arena of the court and criminal charges lead to justice for both the accused and the community? The charge to all of us is very clear.

We must make it possible for judges to spend more time judging by giving them professional help for administrative tasks. We must change the criminal court system, provide the manpower—in terms of court staffs, prosecutors, defense counsel—to bring about speedier trials and appeals.

We must insure the fundamental civil rights of every American—the right to be secure in his home and on the streets. We must make it possible for the civil litigant to get a hearing on his case at least in the same year that he files it.

And we must make it possible for each community to train its police to carry out their duties, using the most modern methods of detection and crime prevention. We must make it possible for the convicted criminal to receive constructive training while in confinement, instead of what he receives now usually—an advanced course in crime.

The time has come to repudiate once and for all the idea that prisons are warehouses for human rubbish; our correctional systems must be changed to make them places that will correct and educate; and, of special concern to this conference, we must strengthen the state court systems to enable them to fulfill their historic role as the tribunals of justice nearest and most responsive to the people.

The Federal Government has been treating the process of justice as a matter of the highest priority, as you know. In the budget for the coming year, the Law Enforcement Assistance Administration will be enabled to vigorously expand its aid to state and local governments. Close to one half billion dollars a year will now go to strengthen local efforts to reform court procedures, police methods, correctional action, and other related needs. And in my new special revenue-sharing proposal, law enforcement is an area that receives increased attention and greater funding—in a way that permits states and localities to determine their own priorities.

The District of Columbia which, as you know, is the only American city under direct Federal supervision, now has legislation and funding which enables us to reorganize its court system, provides enough judges to bring accused to trial promptly, and protects the public against habitual offenders. We hope this new reform legislation may serve as an example to other communities throughout the nation.

And today I am endorsing the concept of a suggestion that I understand Chief Justice Burger will make to you tomorrow: the establishment of a National Center for the State Courts.

This will make it possible for state courts to conduct research into problems of procedure, administration, and training for state and local judges and their administrative personnel; it could serve as a clearinghouse for the exchange of information about state court problems and reforms. A Federal Judicial Center along these lines, as you know, already exists for the Federal court system. It has proved its worth; the time is overdue for state courts to have such a facility available for them. I will look to the conferees here in Williamsburg to assist in making recommendations as to how best to create such a center, and what will be needed for its initial funding.

I can pledge our cooperation in what you recommend.

Speaking for the executive branch of the Federal Government, we will continue to try to help in every way. But the primary impetus for reforming and improving the judicial process must come from within the system itself. Your presence here is evidence of your deep concern; and my presence here bears witness to the concern of all of the American people regardless of party, occupation, race, or economic condition, for the overhaul of a system of justice that has simply been neglected too long....

We shall become a genuinely just society only by "playing the game according to the rules," and when the rules become outdated or are shown to be unfair, by lawfully and peaceably changing those rules.

The genius of our system, the life force of the American way, is our ability to hold fast to the rules that we know to be right and to change the rules that we know to be wrong. In that regard, we would all do well to remember our constitutional roles: for the legislatures, to set forth the rules; for the judiciary, to interpret them; for the executive, to carry them out.

The American Revolution did not end two centuries ago; it's a living process. It must constantly be reexamined and reformed. At one and the same time, it is as unchanging as the spirit of laws and as changing as the needs of our people.

We live in a time when headlines are made by those few who want to tear down our institutions, to those who say they defy the law. But we also live in a time when history is made by those who are willing to reform and rebuild our institutions—that can only be accomplished by those who respect the law.

BIBLIOGRAPHY

BOOKS, PAMPHLETS, AND DOCUMENTS

An asterisk (*) preceding a reference indicates that the article or a part of it has been reprinted in this book.

American Assembly. The courts, the public, and the law explosion. [Harry W. Jones: editor] Prentice-Hall. '65.

American Society for Political and Legal Philosophy. Justice; Carl J. Friedrich and John W. Chapman. eds. Atherton Press. '63.

Association of the Bar of the City of New York. Special Committee on Radio, Television and the Administration of Justice. Freedom of the press and fair trial. Columbia University Press. '67.

Baldwin, R. W. Social justice. Pergamon Press. '66.

Beaney, W. M. and others. Perspectives on the Court. Northwestern University Press. '67.

Bergler, Edmund and Meerloo, J. A. M. Justice and injustice; the origin of the sense of justice and its relation to everyday life, the law, and the problems of juvenile delinquency and crime. Grune & Stratton. '63.

Bird, O. A. The idea of justice. (Institute for Philosophical Research. Concepts in Western Thought Series) Praeger. '67.

Bloomstein, M. J. Verdict: the jury system. Dodd. '68.

*Burger, W. E. The state of the Federal judiciary; addresss before the annual meeting of the American Bar Association, St. Louis, August 10, 1970. The Author. Office of the Chief Justice. U.S. Supreme Court Bldg. 1 First St. N.E. Washington, D.C. 20543. '70.

> Also in U.S. News & World Report. 69:68-71. Ag. 24, '70. What's wrong with the courts; the Chief Justice speaks out.

Carter, R. M. and Wilkins, L. T. eds. Probation and parole; selected readings. Wiley. '70.

*Clark, Ramsey. Crime in America; observations on its nature, causes, prevention and control. Simon & Schuster. '70.

> Excerpts. Saturday Review. 53:21-4+. S. 19, '70. Criminal justice in times of turbulence.
> Reprinted in this book: Chapter 18: "Presumed innocent? Bail and preventive detention." p 277-94 of the Pocket Book edition.

Devlin, P. A. D., baron. Trial by jury. 3rd impression with addendum. Stevens. '66.

Downie, Leonard, Jr. Justice denied: the case for reform of the courts. Praeger. '71.

> Excerpts. Current History. 61:82-6+. Ag. '71. Criminal court logjam.

Frank, Jerome. Courts on trial; myth and reality in American justice. Atheneum. '63.

Frank, J. P. American law; the case for radical reform; lectures by John P. Frank upon the dedication of the Earl Warren Legal Center, University of California. Macmillan. '69.
    Review. Saturday Review. 53:34-5. Mr. 21, '70. Martin Mayer.

Friedman, Leon, ed. Southern justice. Pantheon Books. '65.

Friendly, Alfred and Goldfarb, R. L. Crime and publicity; the impact of news on the administration of justice. Twentieth Century Fund. '67.

Glaser, Daniel. The effectiveness of a prison and parole system. abridged ed. Bobbs. '69.

Goldfarb, Ronald. Ransom: a critique of the American bail system. foreword by Arthur J. Goldberg. Harper. '65.

Graham, F. P. The self-inflicted wound. Macmillan. '70.

James, H. I. Children in trouble. McKay. '70.

James, H. I. Crisis in the courts. McKay. '68.

Kalven, Harry, Jr. and Zeisel, Hans. The American jury. University of Chicago Press. '71.

Karlen, Delmar. Judicial administration; The American experience. Butterworth & Co. '70.

Kelsen, Hans. What is justice? justice, law, and politics in the mirror of science; collected essays. University of California Press. '57.

Kennedy, R. F. The pursuit of justice; ed. by Theodore J. Lowi. Harper. '64.

Lobenthal, J. S. Jr. Power and put-on; the law in America. Outerbridge and Dienstfrey. '71. [distributed by Dutton]

Lukas, A. J. The barnyard epithet and other obscenities; notes on the Chicago conspiracy trial. Harper. '70.

Morris, Norval and Hawkins, Gordon. The honest politician's guide to crime control. University of Chicago Press. '70.

Murphy, W. F. and Pritchett, C. H. eds. Courts, judges and politics; an introduction to the judicial process. Random House. '61.

New York (City). Office of the Comptroller. Research and Liaison Unit. Drug addiction and the administration of justice. ['70.] The Unit. 625 Municipal Bldg. New York 10007.

Oaks, D. H. and Lehman, Warren. A criminal justice system and the indigent; a study of Chicago and Cook County. University of Chicago Press. '68.

Payton, B. E. Scapegoat: prejudice/politics/prison. Whitmore Pub. Co. '70.

Pound, Roscoe. Justice according to law. (Westminster College. Green Foundation Lectures, 1950) Yale University Press. '51.

Schur, E. M. Our criminal society; the social and legal sources of crime in America. Prentice-Hall. '69.

Seigenthaler, John, and others. A search for justice. Aurora Pubs. '71.
> *Review article*: New York Times. p 38. Ag. 15, '71. Book casts doubt on justice in U.S.

Sherrill, Robert. Military justice is to justice as military music is to music. Harper. '70.
> *Review.* Newsweek. 75:103+. My. 11, '70. Geoffrey Wolff.

Simon, R. J. The jury and the defense of insanity. Little. '67.

Stone, Julius. Human law and human justice. Stanford University Press. '65.

Sussmann, F. B. Law of juvenile delinquency; the laws of the forty-eight states. (Legal Almanac Ser.) Oceana. '50.

Sutherland, A. E. The law and one man among many. (Wisconsin. Univ. School of Law. Oliver S. Rundell Lectures) University of Wisconsin Press. '56.

Sykes, G. M. and Drabek, T. E. comps. Law and the lawless; a reader in criminology. Random House. '69.

Taylor, Telford. Nuremberg and Vietnam: an American tragedy. (New York Times Book) Quadrangle Books. '70.

Tillich, Paul. Love, power and justice; ontological analyses and ethical applications; given as Firth lectures in Nottingham, England, and as Sprunt lectures in Richmond, Virginia. Oxford University Press. '54.

United States. Commission on Civil Rights. Law enforcement; a report on equal protection in the South. Supt. of Docs. Washington, D.C. 20025. '65.

United States. House of Representatives. Committee on the Judiciary. Subcommittee No. 5. Circuit court executives: hearing, July 8, 1970 on H.R. 17901 and H.R. 17906, proposals to improve judicial machinery by providing for the appointment of a circuit executive for each judicial circuit. 91st Congress, 2d session. The Committee. Washington, D.C. 20515. '70.

United States. National Commission on Law Observance & Enforcement. Report on police, No. 14. Supt. of Docs. Washington, D. C. 20025. '31.

United States. Senate. Committee on the District of Columbia. Court management study: I, Report of the Committee on the Administration of Justice to the Judicial Council of the District of Columbia circuit; II, A program for improved management in the District of Columbia courts: report, parts 1-2; summary. 91st Congress, 2d session. Supt. of Docs. Washington, D.C. 20025. My. '70.

United States. Task Force on Juvenile Delinquency. Task Force report: juvenile delinquency and youth crime; report on juvenile justice and consultants' papers. Supt. of Docs. Washington, D.C. 20025. '67.

United States. Task Force on the Police. Task Force report: the police. Supt. of Docs. Washington, D.C. 20025. '67.

PERIODICALS

*America. 123:310-11. O. 24, '70. High cost of criminal laws.

America. 125:309-11. O. 23, '71. The case for trial by jury. J. M. Murtagh.

American Bar Association Journal. 56:755-9. Ag. '70. The proposed National court assistance act. F. M. Armstrong.

American Scholar. 39:445-62. Summer '70. Campus rights and responsibilities: a role for lawyers? Nathan Glazer.

American Scholar. 40:686-90. Autumn '71. Social change and the police. P. V. Murphy.

American Scholar. 40:622-6. Autumn '71. Toward juvenile justice; address, July 12, 1971. Birch Bayh.

American West. 7:4-47. Ja. '70. Variations on a theme of law and order; symposium, with introduction by W. H. Hutchinson.

Atlanta Magazine. 10:41-50+. S. '70. The badge of caution. [New court rulings, the need to protect the legal rights of all, the rising crime rate, the overloaded courts—all contribute to dilemmas in the U.S. system of law; what needs to be done.] William Schemmel.

Atlantic. 227:45-52. Mr. '71. Kind and usual punishment in California. Jessica Mitford.

Christian Century. 87:1286. O. 28, '70. Imprisoning the poor. D. G. Shockley.

Christian Century. 88:213-14. F. 17, '71. Ethicists examine conspiracy laws.

*Christian Science Monitor. p 17. Je. 5, '71. The culprit: criminal or climate? R. L. Strout.

Columbia Survey of Human Rights Law. 2:52-90. '69/'70. The Federal Jury Selection Act of 1968: a critique. J. L. Levin.

Commentary. 51:31-40. Ja., 14+. My. '71. Judging the Chicago trial. A. M. Bickel.

Commentary. 51:69-71. Mr. '71. Advocate. Dorothy Rabinowitz.

Commonweal. 93:139-40. N. 6, '70. Whose law? Whose order? [Commission on civil rights report]

Commonweal. 93:371-2. Ja. 15, '71. Getting busted in New York; night court is easily the greatest show in town. Philip Tracy.

Congressional Digest. 50:193-224. Ag. '71. This month's feature: the question of revising the jury system.

*Current History. 60:327-34. Je. '71. Development of local and state law enforcement. V. W. Peterson.

*Current History. 61:20-6. Jl. '71. Pretrial and nontrial in the lower criminal courts. R. M. Pious.

Current History. 61:97-104+. Ag. '71. British, French and American systems of justice compared. B. C. Canon.

Current History. 61:65-104+. Ag. '71. Improving justice in America; symposium.

Current History. 61:92-6+. Ag. '71. Jury system reform. A. S. Nanes.

*Editorial Research Reports. 1, no 21:403-22. Je. 3, '70. Reform of the courts. R. C. Deans.

*Fortune. 82:110-14+. Ag. '70. Only radical reform can save the courts. Jeremy Main.

Good Housekeeping. 171:12+. Jl. '70. Rescue of Donald and Richard [boys saved from an adult prison]. William Hartley and Ellen Hartley.

Journal of Politics. 32:599-627. Ag. '70. Crises, politics and Federal judicial reform: the Administrative Office Act of 1939. P. G. Fish.

Judicature. 54:99-103. O. '70. A development program for court administration; address. Herbert Brownell.

Life. 68:34. F. 27, '70. Justice in Chicago; an ominous farce.

Life. 69:2A, 18-25. Ag. 7, '70. Logjam in our courts [with editorial comment]. Dale Wittner.

*Life. 70:56-8+. Mr. 12, '71. "I have nothing to do with justice"; brilliant and cynical, a Legal Aid lawyer wins freedom for thousands of muggers, rapists and thieves. James Mills.

Nation. 210:490-2. Ap. 27, '70. Night thoughts of a police chief. J. P. Kimble.

Nation. 210:770-1. Je. 29, '70. Lawlessness and disorder.

*Nation. 210:774-85. Je. 29, '70. Law and order 1970 [Congressional Conference on Justice in America]; with comment by Ramsey Clark. R. L. Smith.

*Nation. 211:365-8. O. 19, '70. Overkill at the Silver dollar; Chicanos in Los Angeles. E. H. Lopez.

Nation. 211:420-1. N. 2, '70. Whose law? Whose order? [editorial]

Nation. 211:431-4. N. 2, '70. Justice in violent times. Stanley Mosk.

Nation. 211:495-6. N. 16, '70. Boondocks jail the future [high bail for Negroes in Homer, La.]. N. C. Chriss.

Nation. 211:587-91. D. 7, '70. Justice in a torn nation; interview with Ramsey Clark, ed. by R. G. Sherrill.

Nation. 211:582. D. 7, '70. Law 'n' order in Dallas; case of four black students from the University of California.

Nation. 211:612. D. 14, '70. Fortresses of the law; courtroom security.

Nation. 211:687-90. D. 28, '70. Trading law for order. R. C. Eckhardt.

Nation. 211:690-1. D. 28, '70. Can a black be acquitted? N. C. Chriss.

Nation. 212:482-3. Ap. 19, '71. Captain and the President [Aubrey Daniel's letter to the President in contrast to the President's TV address of April 7].

Nation. 212:514-15. Ap. 26, '71. Sovereign F.B.I.

Nation. 213:166. S. 6, '71. Balance sheet on justice.

National Review. 22:480. My. 5, '70. Repression, U.S.A. W. F. Buckley, Jr.

New Republic. 162:11-12. Ap. 25, '70. Grass & the brass. David Sanford.

New Republic. 163:4. O. 17, '70. TRB from Washington: Organized crime control act of 1970.

New Republic. 163:7-8. O. 31, '70. Canada can, can we?

New Republic. 163:4. O. 31, '70. TRB from Washington: One-eyed justice.

New Republic. 163:14-17. N. 7, '70. Kent State gag; report of the Ohio special grand jury. David Sanford.

New Republic. 164:12-17. Ap. 17, '71. Privacy and the third-party bug. Nathan Lewin.

*New Republic. 164:24-5. My. 29, '71. Advocates: Legal services, inc. R. M. Hall, Jr.

New York Times. p 1+. Mr. 12, '71. President urges "genuine reform" of court system. F. P. Graham.

New York Times. p 1+. Mr. 19, '71. Rules for Tombs ordered by U.S. A. H. Lubasch.

New York Times. p 39. Mr. 19, '71. Dan & Phil & Edgar & John. W. V. Casey.

New York Times. p 1+. Ap. 16, '71. Berrigan case subpoenas served on 10 by the F.B.I. Bill Kovach.

New York Times. p 22. Ap. 21, '71. U.S. seeking a new indictment replacing one in Berrigan case. Bill Kovach.

New York Times. p 1+. O. 3, '71. Justices face new issues tomorrow as term opens. F. P. Graham.

New York Times. p 109. D. 8, '71. Burger bids prison heads give inmates some voice. Lesley Oelsner.

New York Times Magazine. p 28-9+. Mr. 1, '70. Brief for preventive detention. R. L. Goldfarb.

*New York Times Magazine. p 30-1+. Ap. 5, 114-15 My. 3, '70. What to do when the judge is put up against the wall. Louis Nizer.

New York Times Magazine. p 30-1+. My. 24, '70. Same justice can be both a strict and a loose constructionist. Anthony Lewis.

New York Times Magazine. p. 32-3+. Ag. 23, '70. Law professor behind ASH, SOUP, PUMP, and CRASH. J. A. Page.
    Reply. New York Times Magazine. p 33. S. 27, '70. R. H. Quinn.

New Yorker. 46:38-9. O. 10, '70. Voir dire; selecting a jury for the Panther 21 trial.

*New Yorker. 46:76-84. F. 6, '71. Annals of law: be just and fear not. E. J. Kahn, Jr.

Newsweek. 75:22-4. Mr. 2, '70. Judgment in Chicago.

Newsweek. 76:18-20+. Ag. 31, '70. U.S. military justice on trial.

Newsweek. 77:35+. Ap. 19, '71. What's bugging Boggs.

Redbook. 136:74-5+. F. '71. What are tomorrow's lawyers thinking today? Walter Goodman.

Saturday Review. 53:31+. F. 21, '70. Protesters, police, and politicians. J. M. Unruh.

Saturday Review. 53:26. My. 2, '70. White House and free speech. W. I. Roberts.

*Saturday Review. 53:26+. N. 21, '70. Law-and-order issue. Peter Schrag.

*Saturday Review. 54:17-19+. F. 13, '71. The roots of lawlessness. H. S. Commager.

Saturday Review. 54:19-22. Ag. 7, '71. Neglected values locked into the law. Sidney Hyman.

*Senior Scholastic. 97:7-16. D. 14, '70. Is justice at bay? [special issue]
    Reprinted in this book: The U.S. court system under fire. John Starke. p 7-10.

Time. 95:38-9. F. 23, '70. Chicago trial: a loss for all.

Time. 95:61. Ap. 6, '70. Bias in the jury box.

Time. 95:65. Ap. 27, '70. Dissent through the courts.

Time. 97:15-16. Ap. 19, '71. Bugging J. Edgar Hoover.

Time. 97:16-17. My. 3, '71. Of Hoover and Clark.

Time. 98:71-2. O. 18, '71. Judge for a day; antidote to court congestion.

Trans-Action. 8:10+. Ja. '71. Death takes a holiday. W. J. Lassers.

U.S. News & World Report. 68:6-7. Mr. 2, '70. Unfinished business of the Chicago trial.

U.S. News & World Report. 68:20-1. Mr. 16, '70. There has been a terrible breakdown in criminal justice; excerpts from interview, February 15, 1970; ed. by J. McCaffrey. E. B. Williams.

U.S. News & World Report. 68:55-8. Mr. 23, '70. Citizens' war on crime; spreading across U.S.

U.S. News & World Report. 68:41-2. My. 11, '70. Behind the turmoil at Yale: black power and the courts.

U.S. News & World Report. 69:40-3. Jl. 20, '70. How to stop rise in crime; interview. Leon Jaworski.

U.S. News & World Report. 69:94-8. S. 21, '70. What's needed to speed up justice; interview with E. B. Williams.

U.S. News & World Report. 69:32-6+. D. 14, '70. Interview with Chief Justice Warren E. Burger.

*U.S. News & World Report. 70:65. Ja. 11, '71. Action to help clear logjam in courts.

*U.S. News & World Report. 70:55. Ja. 18, '71. Death penalty on way out? [proposed new Federal criminal code]

U.S. News & World Report. 70:37. Mr. 22, '71. Speeding up justice: President's plan.

*Vital Speeches of the Day. 36:354-9. Ap. 1, '70. Case for pretrial detention; address, January 30, 1970. R. G. Kleindienst.

Vital Speeches of the Day. 37:301-4. Mr. 1, '71. Respect for the law and lawyers; address, February 6, 1971. Philip Lesly.

Vital Speeches of the Day. 37:374-6. Ap. 1, '71. Look at our judicial system; address. R. S. Ayala.

*Vital Speeches of the Day. 37:574-6. Jl. 1, '71. Criminal violence: how about the victim; address, May 12, 1971. T. L. Sendak.

Vital Speeches of the Day. 37:615-18. Ag. 1, '71. Legal services: reform in the seventies; address, April 15, 1971. Robert Taft, Jr.

*Weekly Compilation of Presidential Documents. 6:1018-20. Ag. 10, '70. The President's remarks to reporters at the Federal Office Building, Denver, Colorado. August 3, 1970. R. M. Nixon.

    Excerpts. U.S. News & World Report. 69:70. Ag. 17, '70. Nixon's plea: stop making heroes out of criminals.

*Weekly Compilation of Presidential Documents. 7:460-6. Mr. 15, '71. The President's remarks at the opening session of the meeting in Williamsburg, Virginia, of the National Conference on the Judiciary, March 11, 1971.

    Excerpts. New York Times. p 18. Mr. 12, '71.